The Happy Intercessor

The Happy Intercessor

BENI JOHNSON

© Copyright 2009 – Beni Johnson

All rights reserved. This book is protected by the copyright laws of the United States of America. This book may not be copied or reprinted for commercial gain or profit. The use of short quotations or occasional page copying for personal or group study is permitted and encouraged. Permission will be granted upon request. Unless otherwise identified, Scripture quotations are from the New King James Version. Copyright © 1982 by Thomas Nelson, Inc. Scripture quotations marked NASB are taken from the NEW AMERICAN STANDARD BIBLE®, Copyright © 1960, 1962, 1963, 1968, 1971, 1972, 1973, 1975, 1977, 1995 by the Lockman Foundation. Used by permission. All rights reserved. Scripture quotations marked TM are taken from The Message. Copyright © 1993, 1994, 1995, 1996, 2000, 2001, 2002. Used by permission of NavPress Publishing Group. Scripture quotations marked NIV are taken from the HOLY BIBLE, NEW INTERNATIONAL VERSION®, Copyright © 1973, 1978, 1984 International Bible Society. Used by permission of Zondervan. All rights reserved. All emphasis within Scripture quotations is the author's own. Please note that Destiny Image's publishing style capitalizes certain pronouns in Scripture that refer to the Father, Son, and Holy Spirit, and may differ from some publishers' styles. Take note that the name satan and related names are not capitalized. We choose not to acknowledge him, even to the point of violating grammatical rules.

DESTINY IMAGE® PUBLISHERS, INC.

P.O. Box 310, Shippensburg, PA 17257-0310

"Speaking to the Purposes of God for this Generation and for the Generations to Come."

This book and all other Destiny Image, Revival Press, Mercy Place, Fresh Bread, Destiny Image Fiction, and Treasure House books are available at Christian bookstores and distributors worldwide.

For a U.S. bookstore nearest you, call 1-800-722-6774.

For more information on foreign distributors, call 717-532-3040.

Or reach us on the Internet: www.destinyimage.com

ISBN 10: 0-7684-2753-3

ISBN 13: 978-0-7684-2753-0

For Worldwide Distribution, Printed in the U.S.A.

3 4 5 6 7 8 9 10 11 / 13 12 11 10 09

DEDICATION

This book I'm dedicating to my children and their spouses.

I am the most blessed woman. I have learned so much from them. Their love for life has been an inspiration and joy to me. My prayer for them is that they would always keep the super and the natural in their lives and in their love for God.

Special love to my grandchildren, Kennedy, Selah, Haley, Judah, Téa, Diego, Bradon, and Isabella; watching you discover the spirit realm as you grow has been and is going to be the best part of my life. As poppa says, "I love you massive!"

ACKNOWLEDGMENTS

I would like to thank my husband for being the greatest man alive. You are amazing! My life with you has been beyond my dreams. You have always let me be me, and you have always let me soar with Jesus. You have supported me in this project all the way, but most of all you have supported me in my life, this happy adventure. I love you with all my heart!

A huge thanks to all my wild, wonderful friends; we are crazy for Jesus. Thanks for your faithful prayer covering!

Special thanks to Judy, who helped with this project; your input means so much to me. Pam, thank you. You are an amazing editor. And Erica, you made this project so fun. Thanks for pulling it out of me.

Thanks to Jeremy who had a dream about this book and saw the title in the dream. It all came together when you told me. Way to go!

ENDORSEMENTS

I love this book! It may be the best book on prayer ever. *The Happy Intercessor is* alive with Presence. Learn the secret of the secret place: how to capture the heartbeat of heaven and pray it into our world—but be happy while you're at it. The first opportunity I had to fellowship with Beni she invited me for a walk around her city. As we went over the now famous Sundial Bridge mentioned in Chapter 4 (where we find out how to "own your city") the thing that impacted me most was her joy. It was not noisy joy. And it felt like Heaven listened when she spoke. Beni seemed thoroughly at rest, confident in a *big* God, so aware of the world around, and so alive with the sense that when she prayed earth obeyed. I know now that she got that through her journey into God's heart. If you live it, you can give it away. That is what

Beni does in this book. *The Happy Intercessor* is a gift for every person hungry to know God face to face. This book is a must for every person seeking significance. From classical theology with a down-to-earth prophetic twist to mastering the mystical realm, *The Happy Intercessor* is practical, pragmatic, and personal. Take this book and lay down in God...I think you'll find you're soaring!

Bonnie Chavda
Sr. Assoc. Pastor, All Nations Church
Cofounder, The Watch of the Lord
Charlotte, NC

I have read no less than 40 books on intercession. Some challenged me to pray more, others helped me to see God's design for prayer, but few kept my rapt attention like Beni Johnson's *The Happy Intercessor*. This is one of the most interesting books on intercession I have ever read. Beni has the unique ability to blend the heavenly with the practical through her own life stories and biblical insight. This is a must read for every person called to intercession, especially if you are having trouble being consistent at it.

John Paul Jackson
Founder, Streams Ministries International
Author, *Unmasking the Jezebel Spirit*

I have known Beni Johnson for more than thirty years. I have watched her relationship with God grow into one of the most beautiful love stories that has ever been told. Just spending a few minutes with her will cause you to hunger for more intimacy with the Father and will remind you of your first love. *The Happy Intercessor* is more than a good book on prayer; it is a Holy Spirit journey into the very heart of the Father. This book could revolutionize the way you relate to God on every level. Let the journey begin!

Kris Vallotton
Cofounder, Bethel School of Supernatural Ministry
Author, *The Supernatural Ways of Royalty*
and *Developing a Supernatural Lifestyle*

This is a book that makes intercession engaging, exciting, and dare I say...exhilarating? I think it can spark a revolution among people like me who need fresh, innovative insight into how to pray "without ceasing" and still be energized. With this book in hand, we can recruit an army of "killer sheep" to police the heavens in every community and the top of every mountain of influence...and enjoy the battle!

Lance Wallnau
Founder, Lance Learning Group

The Happy Intercessor is a one-of-a-kind manuscript, providing valuable insight into the often misunderstood realm of intercession. Like its author, this extraordinary book is real, down to earth, and refreshingly honest. *Happy Intercessor* skillfully captures the true heart of intercession in a way that is uncomplicated, yet powerful in application.

Larry Randolph
Founder, Larry Randolph Ministries
Author, *Spirit Talk*, *The Coming Shift*,
and *User Friendly Prophecy*

TABLE OF CONTENTS

FOREWORD

Writing an endorsement or a foreword for a book is a great honor. This is especially true when you know the author and have seen how the message she has written has been lived out in her life. That being the case, I've never been more honored to write on behalf of another author than I have with this one: my wife.

Any time I introduce Beni in my travels or present her teaching CDs, I mention that she is a sign and a wonder —*she is a happy intercessor*. That comment usually gets a laugh because it is one area of church life where harshness, intolerance, and depression have been considered the price of admission. That nervous laughter also reveals a hope that it could be different. We have discovered, as a church, that it can and must be different.

I was there when the prophetic declaration was made over her life about becoming an intercessor. We both had been exposed to intercessors who made us want anything but that calling in life. Their *burden*, which we discovered later was just a fancy word for depression, was not a very inviting image for those of us who were truly wanting to learn how to pray. But she knew enough not to reject the word.

I remember the night my wife was changed from timid to bold—from a *behind the scenes* kind of person to being in front, giving direction. It happened in one night. She had an encounter with the Lord in Toronto in which she shook like a dishrag. It was fearful and amazing to watch. All fear of man and intimidation seemed to be shaken right out of her. A lioness was born that night.

Her journey in intercession began the best way possible. She was a lover of God first and foremost. And that became the context for all her learning. Sometimes you just don't know the keys and profound principles for bringing a breakthrough in an area, but you can always take time to love God. That is her story. While Beni's insights and experiences are true and profound, they were not learned because of a desire to be powerful. They are all born out of the desire just to know and love God with every possible breath. I believe that to be the secret to effective prayer—to love God, period. Because loving God develops a partnership. And it's much more fun to pray with God than merely to pray to Him.

Bill Johnson

THE JOURNEY

I was not always an intercessor. But I still remember the first time those words were spoken over me over 20 years ago. My husband, Bill, and I were pastoring a church in Weaverville, California. We had asked our friend, prophet Dick Joyce, to come and minister at the church. Dick called me forward to prophesy over me and said, "You are called to intercession. Not for this season but for a season coming."

I remember that, on my way up to receive that word, I whispered to the Lord, "I will take any gift but intercession." But somehow, even when Dick spoke those words over me, I remember that I was not surprised. It was almost as though my spirit already knew it was coming. At the time, it was Dick's words, "not for this season but for a season coming" that brought me the most comfort because, at the time, I did not want to be an intercessor.

I knew then that sometimes it is necessary to put those kinds of prophetic words "up on a shelf" for a season. I remember that someone had told me once that if you received a prophetic word that did not line up, you were just supposed to "put it up on a shelf" and tuck it away until it was time for it to come to pass. I knew this was a right word from the Lord, but the timing would come later. And that was OK with me. I needed time to really understand what intercession was.

You may be wondering why I would whisper to the Lord that I did not want to receive the gift of intercession. You see, I grew up in a church where the "intercessors" did not look like happy people a lot of the time. From my small perspective, all those who were intercessors were the ones who walked around with what looked to me like very heavy burdens. The intercessors always looked sad to me, and I don't remember seeing them smile.

As I got older, I remember thinking, "I do not want to be an intercessor." I had grown up thinking that, if you were an intercessor, you had to carry heavy burdens around all the time because that was all that I had seen. I did not know that it was possible for intercessors to be happy. I had a lot to learn.

I Was the "Quiet One"

For many years, I did not know that I was an intercessor. When I look back now, I can see all the signs: I spent so much time carrying so many feelings inside of me and internalizing them as if they were my own. For example, I would often walk into a room filled with people and start feeling and hearing their thoughts—thoughts which were often very negative.

Not realizing, however, that all of those feelings that I was experiencing were the gift that the Bible calls "discernment of spirits," I would carry those burdensome emotions as my own instead of releasing them in prayer. As a result, I became depressed. I became a "quiet one."

You see, as a child, I was told that I was shy. My parents didn't do this, but others did. Unfortunately, because so many people told me that I was shy, over and over, I began to think that I was shy. I took those words as truth. I agreed with those words and received them as my identity.

Sadly, being shy eventually became a stronghold in my life that controlled me. I remember being so afraid of people that it became difficult for me to talk out loud. I was afraid of saying the wrong thing, afraid that I would forget what I was going to say in the middle of a sentence. I also remember how tormenting it was for me if I had to speak in front of people. I would rather take an "F" on an oral test than get up in front of people.

My Walk with God

My mother has told me that, even when I was a very young girl, I would go to her and have her pray with me about everything. She said I would ask her to pray for me about my "owies" or kids in the neighborhood who had gotten hurt. I had no idea at the time that it was my mercy gift working.

Going to my mom to pray gave me release from these things. When I would pray, it would help me to release my feelings and give them to God. I remember that I often had a sense of what other people were feeling and going through, even people I did not know. Sometimes I was even aware of unspoken thoughts and emotions that people were feeling all around me.

In my teen years, I was still caught in this place of feeling a lot of feelings that were not my own. The problem was that I had stopped praying. I forgot what to do with all those feelings, so I carried them as mine. That led to a lot of depression in my earlier years.

Gratefully, when I turned 16, I had an encounter with God that changed my life. For the two years before the encounter, I had pretty much led my own life and done my own thing, and it brought me to a place of desperation. One night in church, there was a call to come forward to give your life to God, and I did, and I let it all out. I remember going before the Lord that night, crying out to Him and saying to the Lord, "All I want is you." I remember asking the Lord to take my life that night. And He did.

After that encounter, I did not do anything unless I prayed about it. I would go to my closet and open it and ask Jesus what I should wear that day. But I still did not understand my gifting and how to pray. Even though I was going through this amazing time with God in part of my life, I was not releasing to Him all of the things that I was feeling and picking up around me. I continued to internalize. I had no one to tell me that the emotions I was feeling inside of me and sensing around me were things that I needed to be praying about.

When I was 17, I went to a discipleship training center for nine months. One of my roommates had a lot of mental instability. I was so concerned for her because I would feel what she was going through, but I did not make a connection that I was actually personally experiencing the same exact things that she was experiencing. I remember being in the room one day with her, and we were both sitting on our beds. Such incredible despair overcame me that I remember feeling as though I wanted to give up on life. I didn't realize, however, that I was actually picking up the mental torment that my roommate was experiencing—feelings that I too had once experienced. I did not know what to do with these tormenting emotions! It did not click, and I had no idea that God was showing me that I was supposed to be praying for her.

Romans 8:28 says, "All things work together for good to those who love God, to those who are the called according to His purpose." Years later, as I began working in ministry, I would realize that God allowed the experiences of my past to show me the *purpose* for which He has truly called me to be used today.

A Wife and a Mother

I met Bill at Bethel Church in 1969, when his father was the pastor of the church. We met during the Jesus Movement, got married, and spent five years on staff at Bethel before we moved to Weaverville, California to pastor a small church in the mountains. I had a prayer life, but it was just a general prayer life. I prayed for my kids and my family or things that were going on in the church. I prayed because I thought that was what I was supposed to do. I did not pray out of relationship with the Holy Spirit.

For the most part, when we lived in Weaverville, I spent my time as a mother of young children. For me, finding time to pray was extremely difficult. I remember that my prayer time was usually during doing the dishes, or else I had to wake up very early to read my Bible and pray. To be honest, it felt like more of an obligation than a desire. There was still something deep within me that truly desired to be with God, but because of my busy schedule, I would never really take the time to pursue that deep calling to deep. Looking back, I can see now that there was a pull to go deeper with God, but I did not know where to go or how to get there. And then renewal came.

A Renewed Life

In 1995, renewal came to our church in Weaverville. It was a time of great refreshing and joy. It was also a time when the Holy Spirit stirred up my heart, releasing me to be who I am. A brand new season was coming. In this time of stirring, I felt Him speak to me a word that would change my life. I heard these words, "I want you to carry joy and intercession." My first thought was, "Is that possible?" I still only saw intercession as a depressed way of living.

With renewal, people were experiencing so much freedom. I had two different experiences during that time that I would call life-changing encounters with God. One of those experiences happened in Toronto, at John and Carol Arnott's church, Toronto Airport Christian Fellowship (TACF). My parents, my husband, and I were attending a conference there on the Father's Blessing, which was the pulse of the whole outpouring there at TACF. After one of the meetings, Bill and I got up to go and walked to the back of the room where there were people everywhere on the floor, much laughter, and Holy Spirit drunkenness. Acts 2:15 says, "For these are not drunk, as you suppose, since it is *only* the third hour of the day." When the Holy Spirit's power hit the disciples in the upper room, they looked and acted like they were drunk. Have you ever noticed that drunken people don't care what other people think about what they are doing at that moment? Well, there was such a man at that meeting that night. We noticed him staggering around the back, laying his hands on people. As he did, they would fall to the ground. God was using that man as a Holy Spirit conduit. Some would laugh with Holy Spirit laughter; others would shake under the power of the Holy Spirit. I looked over at him, and we made eye contact, and he headed my way. I had my arm in Bill's arm, but when the man got over to me, he reached out with one finger and touched my arm. I immediately fell to the ground and began shaking violently. Bill had to let go of my arm. For 20 minutes or so, I shook so hard. At one point, a woman came over to me and asked if I was in good shape. I told her I was, and she just said, "Then, more Lord." And off I went again. It finally subsided a little so that I could get up. But I needed help back to the room.

The next day, we went back to the morning session. As the speaker began speaking something about the Father's love, I felt the presence of God and began to cry. I asked the Lord what had gone on the night before. "What was that all about?" I heard these words: "I was shaking out of you the strongholds of your life and birthing who you are." From that day on, the fear that had guided my life left. The stronghold had been broken. I became a different person through that unusual encounter with God.

Now, I have to tell you that the devil doesn't just sit back and say, "Oh, I can't tempt her anymore." No, he tries to come and get me to make agreement with him. The devil wants us to agree with our old lifestyle patterns. Once we agree with him, he has control again. The devil will allow a familiar spirit to come to us and get us to go back to thinking old ways, but now we are equipped with a supernatural strength to say, "No."

So when a familiar spirit, such as self pity, comes and tries to get us to agree and say, "Yes, that's the way I am," we can now say (because the stronghold has been removed), "No, that is not who I am anymore." I felt as though God had given me a power tool for my life and the strength to use it against the lies from the devil.

Right after this experience in Toronto, I had another life-changing experience. I was at a women's retreat in Mt. Shasta, California. I remember sitting in the back of the room during the worship. I was minding my own business, and Holy Spirit showed up, and I began to cry, the kind of crying that comes from way down deep inside of you. A friend came over to me and asked if I was OK and if I knew what was happening to me. All I knew was that this was God, that something was happening to me, and that it was very deep. I couldn't stop crying. I began to feel like something was being pulled out of me and that something was being activated in me.

After that night, everything began to change. I actually felt like a new person, like my personality had gone through a change. Boldness had come over me. I found that, for the next several months, all I could do was cry. It wasn't a sad cry but a cry that came from a new love that I had found. Every time I would think about God and His goodness or someone would talk about what

God was doing or even mention the name of Jesus, I would begin crying. I was falling in love with the Holy Spirit.

Because the renewal brought refreshing and the Father's heart was being poured out, I found myself, like so many others, lost in His amazing presence. I would go into a deep place of intimacy with Him. I had never experienced anything like this in my whole life of being a believer. I had been raised in the church, and loving God was all that I knew. But this was different. At first it scared me because it was so deep and very intense. I didn't know if this was right. Nobody had told me about this. What was it?

Before I experienced this new level of freedom with the Lord, leading groups and Bible studies had been torture. But this all began to change. I began to see myself as a completely different person. I began to see myself as no longer shy and no longer introverted. I did not care what people thought about me anymore. I remember that, all of a sudden, it became really easy to get up and share Jesus and to share testimonies and to talk about what God was doing. I no longer felt torture related to getting up and talking in front of people; there was such a freedom. I, along with those in the Bible studies and groups I was leading, felt like we were in the midst of a Holy Ghost party. Everyone was getting set free and getting full of joy.

Carrying Joy and Intercession

At this point, my prayer life really began to change. My prayer life was not so much about asking for things anymore but just about wanting to be with the Lord. And I would just worship Him for an hour or more at a time. Music has played a vital part in the personal renewal of my life. I am able to tap into His presence through the tool of worship music. So I would put a worship CD on, sit in God's presence, and enjoy Him. His presence was deep inside of me, in my spirit man.

This happened for a year in Weaverville, and then we moved to Redding to pastor at Bethel. In this whole process of renewal, I was enjoying the presence of God. I was enjoying Him and Him alone. In this process, I began experiencing something unusual. I began seeing pictures of people's faces. I would see cities and towns. I would see situations and problems, and I would find myself, out of that place of intimacy, crying out to God for resolution in the things that I was seeing. I remember one time, after God showed me something, saying, "Oh God, that is such a good idea. Go do that there; take care of that there." It was such a new experience—being able to tap into that deep place of God. I did not realize at the time that I was experiencing true intercession—how it is supposed to be. To be honest, I kind of fell into it.

Around that time, Bethel began to move into renewal. It actually happened one night when my husband called people down that just wanted to be renewed and refreshed. Many people came forward, and we began praying for them. We went over to pray for one lady, and all I can say is that God apprehended this woman in that moment. Bill and I looked at each other and said, "There it is." We knew that renewal had come to Bethel and that the church would never be the same. I looked at the woman's husband and told him, "She will never be the same." Looking back, she has never been the same, and neither has the church.

There was immediate fruit in the woman's life. She was very intimidated by the pastors' wives and was never able to come up and talk with them. That night she came right up to me and just began telling me what God had done for her. She had never been able to just crawl up into the Father's arms and let Him love her, and that happened for her that night. Feeling that love of God completely changed her life.

After that, many people began getting touched by God. We would line people up on Sunday nights after the meetings, and we would see people fall over in the Spirit. And after their experience with God, they would be completely different. Their lives would be completely changed; there would be more freedom, both emotionally and physically. I remember one night walking up to a young lady who was waiting for prayer, and I found out that she was a missionary who had been on the mission field for two years. She had just come home and was absolutely exhausted and burned out from ministry. I began to pray for her, and she fell on the floor under the power of God. For an hour I sat with her on the floor and watched God completely, radically change her life. She laughed; she cried. I laughed; I cried. We laughed and cried together. After an hour, she got up completely different, a brand new person. She no longer had the exhaustion or the depression. She still lives out of that place of freedom today.

Capturing the Heartbeat of Heaven

In 1999, we launched the Bethel School of Supernatural Ministry. We started the school because we wanted to train up a generation that walks in "revival culture." People who walk in revival culture walk in signs and wonders and the prophetic. They do all the stuff that Jesus did when He walked on this planet. It has been so exciting to watch the students come to our school and to see their lives radically changed. I began to watch God raise up a generation that would give themselves completely to Him.

In the midst of all of these happenings, I began to see myself as an intercessor. My definition for being an *intercessor* is "capturing the heartbeat of Heaven and declaring or praying that into my world. It's true agreement with Heaven." And this is what began to happen in my life. God began to give us strategies on how to pray to affect an entire region. We began praying over the land for healing, and from there, it has expanded to going all over the world to pray. Since this time, I have raised teams and taken them to pray for healing over regions. We have gone to many places all over the world. This book is my journey of what God has taught me about prayer and intercession, both in my personal prayer life and in praying over regions. Everything that I have learned has come out of the secret place.

Praying From His Heart

Once renewal hit our church, everything began to change. One of my favorite things that happened during that time was that God began bringing so many of us into that deep, intimate place where we could truly experience His love. At times, many of us felt like His presence was so heavy on us and in us that we would never come out of it. I remember a friend calling me one day and asking me if I would pray for her. She was in His presence, in that deep, far away place, and she needed to be released so that she could cook dinner for her family.

But do not let this one fact escape your notice, beloved, that with the Lord one day is like a thousand years, and a thousand years like one day (2 Peter 3:8 NASB).

So many people were being ushered into His presence during that season in our church. So many, at that time, were caught up into Heaven, into that completeness. We began to hear the heartbeat of Heaven. This depth of His presence was new for many. What we learned was that we were moving into true intercession. There was a mixture of love, joy, and extreme heartbreak. This heartbreak that we would feel was from the extreme, intense love that our Father has for His children all over the world. Like in the story of the prodigal son, we felt the Father missing His children and longing for them to come back to Him and His love. And we found that when we would let ourselves experience the longing of a Heavenly Father, who was desperate to pour His love upon us, that we could almost become "addicted" to His glorious presence. We found that, once we experienced that depth of His love, we desired nothing on Earth more than to be in the presence of our Heavenly Father.

Calling Forth His Desires

In such times, I often *see* faces, places, and situations in my mind's eye. I often feel as if God is showing me things that I need to think about and *brood over* in the way that a mother hen broods over her eggs. Genesis 1:1 says, "Earth was a soup of nothingness, a bottomless emptiness, an inky blackness. God's Spirit brooded like a bird above the watery abyss" (TM). To be honest, most of the time when I am in this place, I just agree. I agree with the plans that God already has for people's lives, for regions, and for the earth. "Yes God, do that God...go there, Father...that's amazing, Lord Jesus." When I pray this way, I feel as though I am praying from His heart and calling into existence the very desires that are already in the heart of God.

In those times, I feel as though I become the very *womb of God*. "He who believes in Me, as the Scripture said, 'From his innermost being will flow rivers of living water'" (John 7:38 NASB). The words *innermost being* come from the word, *koilia*, which means "womb."[1] We are the womb of God. In our intercessions, we are creating and birthing the things of Heaven. We carry the life of the Kingdom within us (see Luke 17:21). It will flow out of us in our intercessions.

No Agendas Required

When any of us go into God's presence, and tap into the realm of Heaven, we position ourselves to receive great breakthrough. One of the things that we need to be careful about is going before God with our own agendas. Sometimes I think we go before God and already have an idea of what we want God to do; so we close ourselves off from receiving from and partnering with God and what He may want to do in the moment. In fact, God may want to do something completely different. It is almost as if we say, "Here God, here is my idea; now do it my way." When we do that, we handcuff God. We are no longer partnering with Him.

Often, when people ask me to pray for them, they come with an agenda—or an idea—of what they want to ask God to do. When I am praying for people and I ask them what they need prayer for, sometimes their requests are not what is on God's agenda for the moment. We need to learn how to be sensitive and move with the Holy Spirit. We need to listen to the heartbeat of God and not always present our ideas to Him. It's not about whether agendas are wrong or right, but when I just want to spend time with God and feel His presence, I don't bring any agenda.

31

I remember one time, while I was praying, a man's face came before me. He was an Asian man. When I saw his face, I began agreeing with God on behalf of this man. To this day, I still do not know anything about this man; nor do I understand what I was praying about concerning him. It could have been an intervention prayer, a prayer that saved that man's life. Or, it could have been that I was praying for a whole people group. Some things will not be known this side of eternity. It is important that we learn to respond to His leading—even when there will be no immediate gratification from seeing an answer in the natural.

Another time, I woke up praying for one of our sons, Brian. I prayed for his safety. Right after I prayed, we got a call from him in the middle of the night telling us that he was driving home from a trip down south. He had fallen asleep at the wheel while driving and had run off the road. He called to tell us that he was OK. I was so thankful that I had been woken up to pray.

Intercession is just the fruit of being with Him. It was birthed in my own heart because of spending time with Him. I go into His presence to love Him, to experience "Spirit-to-spirit"—His Spirit with my spirit. When I experienced this for the first time, I remember just being with Him and feeling our hearts connecting. It felt like my heart was picking up the same heartbeat as His—pouring upon me "liquid love" from His heart. His heart was broken for humanity. Our two hearts are intertwined. When you feel that, when you see His heart broken and His amazing love, your only response can be to pray with burning passion—with compassion for a lost generation.

Whatever God has promised gets stamped with the Yes of Jesus. In Him, this is what we preach and pray, the great

Amen, God's Yes and our Yes together, gloriously evident (2 Corinthians 1:20 TM).

The amazing thing to me is that God is waiting for us to enter into Him. He is longing for us to see His world, to see into that glorious realm of His Kingdom. He wants us to partner with Him for heavenly breakthrough.

God Likes Our Ideas

God's *yes* together with our *yes* is what brings about breakthrough in prayer. I'm continually amazed that God would choose to partner with us. But, at the same time, it makes all the sense in the world that He would want us to join with Him in making history. We are, after all, His children. He is a great and all-powerful God and also a loving and caring Father who, I believe, wants to be involved in our lives. Incredibly, He also wants us to be involved in His Kingdom. He wants us to help build His Kingdom here on earth. Some of the prophetic acts that we do come from the Lord, but I think that some of the things that we do are good ideas that the Father says, "Yeah, that's good."

I am convinced that God likes my ideas. So, when I pray, I pray from a place of security. It is like I go into prayer believing that God is on my side. Let me give you an example. We took a team to Croatia in 2007. It was one of the most amazing prayer trips I've ever been on. One of the places that we planned on going to was a concentration camp outside of Zagreb, the capital of Croatia. During World War II, many Jews, Serbs, Gypsies— anyone who was not a Croat—were put to death. It was brutal. We had joined with our missionary friends and a national pastor and his wife to go there and pray. How do you pray for such a huge, devastating thing? I had been praying, pondering how we could make a difference and help bring healing to a land of much bloodshed. The idea came to get a bottle of wine and have it poured out on the land. We had been praying in one of the towns that morning, and I had honestly wondered if this wine thing was what we were to do. I had mentioned to some of the group that we needed to get a bottle of wine before we left for the concentration camp, but then I purposely dismissed the idea, still thinking that it might not be the right thing to do. One of the women on the team spoke up and said, "Are we going to get the wine before we go to the camp?" "OK. Let's get it," I said.

I hadn't told the national pastors what we were going to do yet. You see, I felt like the pastor and his wife were to pour the wine out on the ground as a prophetic sign of reconciliation prayer. Srecko, the national pastor, is Croatian and his wife, Inas, is Serbian. If you don't know, those were two of the many ethnic groups involved not only in World War II but also in the Bosnian War of the early 1990s. I explained to this wonderful pastor and his wife the idea of pouring out the wine on the ground, and then we prayed together, believing that God would cover the bloodshed over the land with His blood. They held the bottle together and poured. They had never done anything like this before, but they were so gracious. While they poured out the wine, I was watching their 6-year-old son playing. He was so carefree and happy. His bloodline represented two warring ethnic groups. His generation would no longer have the pain of war. There would be healing.

Was this my idea or the Holy Spirit's idea? I don't know. It just felt really right. I feel like our lives can be so intertwined with

God's that our thoughts, feelings, and even what we do are melted together with His. When God made us just the way we are, He liked what He made. He likes everything about us. I believe He enjoys our ideas, and we in turn like His ideas. God chooses us, as He chose David.

First Kings chapter 8 says that God chose David and that it was in David's heart to build a house for the Lord (see 1 Kings 8:16-17). God told David in verse 18, "David...you did well that it was in your heart" (1 Kings 8:18). Wow! That is our God. God chose a man whom He knew would say, "Yes!" And God said, "Yes" to David, and everything else is history. God's *yes* to you and your *yes* to Him are all that is needed.

Staying Focused

When our daughter Leah was expecting her first baby, she asked, with permission from her husband, if I would be the coach for her. I had had three children by natural birth, and she told me, "You're the pro, Mom." It was an honor for me. I told my husband that it was the most amazing experience and the hardest work I've done since I had my own kids.

God is always breaking into our natural world and showing us the spirit realm. That's what happened in this birthing experience with our daughter. In a natural birth, you can invite friends and family into the labor room. Our daughter is a very social being and loved having those friends and family visit up until the time of the birth. As you may know, toward the end of the labor, there is a time that is the most intense. It takes all of your concentration just to make it through the contractions. We were at that place. Whenever a contraction would start, we would release peace over Leah, and then the focus was all on her part to listen to my instructions. One of our friends came into the room at one of those moments and began talking, not really paying attention to the intensity of what was going on. Leah seemed to be OK with it. After the delivery, I asked her about the distraction in the room. She told me that she really didn't notice because she was so focused on my voice and what I was telling her to do. As she told me that, I had a revelation of intercession. When God gives us strategies to pray—you know, the ones that we burn with—we can become so focused on His voice that we don't become distracted. Nothing can take us away from His voice. There were times during delivery of her own child that my daughter and I would lock eyes as well. It was how she got through the intense times. She drew strength from looking into my eyes. There was an intensity or determination in my eyes that she picked up on, which kept her going.

There are times in our lives when we must stay closer, locking onto His words and His vision. God gives us prayer strategies, and we look to Him for focus and understanding on how to pray with results. Then the birthing will come.

By the way, the baby that was born that day to our son-in-law and daughter was named *Judah* (Hebrew for "praise"). The result of our steadfast focus can only be praise for Him.

When I pray from the heart of God, I become so lost in the presence of God that it feels like the only thing I am listening to is the voice of God. In that place, His heart, His plans, His voice become so real that it is almost as if He and I become one. At those times, it feels like I pray with Him. When I am in that place, all I have to do is agree with God and partner with the things that are already on His heart. Those are the times when we pray together and when I begin to co-labor with God through my prayers. Those are the times when I begin to see real break-through, no agenda required.

ENDNOTE

1. Dutch Sheets, *Intercessory Prayer* (Ventura, CA: Regal Books, 1996), 116.

AN OFFENSIVE
LIFESTYLE

Football is an all-American pastime. People are crazy about their teams. Our family is partial to the San Francisco 49ers. There was a time when we would come home from church and couldn't wait to see our favorite quarterback of all time, Joe Montana, work his magic.

On a football team you have a defensive team and an offensive team. The defensive team tries to steal the football from the opposing offensive team. The defensive team will try to figure out the offensive team's strategies and plays. The offensive team, however, has the advantage in that they have the ball. With their skill and different plays, they proceed to carry the football down the field to make a touchdown. The offensive team calls the plays, for they have the ball.

This chapter is about us having the ball. For intercessors, it is extremely important to understand that God has already given us the ball. We are the offensive team. If you don't understand that, if you are not praying from a place of victory, then you will be an intercessor whose prayer life is marked with defeat. You will be one who is always trying to protect what God has given you from the devil's plans or, worse yet, running after the devil and trying to figure out what he is doing. How wrong is that? If you do not understand that God has already given you the ball, you will live in fear and pray from a place of lack.

When Joe Montana would throw that ball down the field, he knew right where it was going—right into the hands of his receiver. It was a thing of beauty. What a picture for us of how to live as Kingdom people who know the plays of Heaven.

A good player will be so focused on his target that it feels like there is no one else around. A good player does not just throw the ball around. Similarly, we can't just throw our prayers around here and there.

Like Joe, we are the offensive team. Offensive teams call the plays. They must have confidence that they are going to win. They have to believe that they will win because they know that they control the ball. As intercessors, as the offensive team, our job is to take the land and not to run around after the enemy trying to steal the ball away from him. The devil lost the ball at Calvary.

As intercessors, we need to always remember that we are playing on an offensive team. On an offensive team, the entire team knows where the ball will go and who will catch it. The entire team knows where to run. They have one focus: to get the touchdown. As intercessors, we *must* listen for the plays that the Lord is calling and pray them in so that the team can catch the ball and make the touchdown. Our job is not to spend all of our time worrying about the enemy's strategies. We are to make the plays that God calls.

A lot of intercessors spend all of their time worrying about what the enemy will do next, but their job is to focus on God and to partner with His plans. As an intercessor, your job is to find out what God wants to do, which is the opposite of what the enemy is saying. Then you begin to pray what God wants. You don't allow the enemy to bring distraction. You have to make a choice not to partner with fear.

This is how intercessors live an offensive lifestyle. They pray according to God's plans, and they pray from a place of victory.

As a result, we are no longer to be children, tossed here and there by waves and carried about by every wind of doctrine, by the trickery of men, by craftiness in deceitful scheming (Ephesians 4:14 NASB).

No Fear Zone

When our third grandchild, Haley, was born, her mommy, Jenn, had an infection, and the doctor had to perform an emergency C-section. As they brought the baby out of surgery and rushed her into NICU, they told us that Haley wasn't responding well. They perform a test on babies when they are first born called the Apgar test. It's a number test, 10 being the best score. Haley's score was 2. We found out later that babies who have a score of 2 usually don't make it. When they gave us this news, we as a family had to make a decision. Would we agree with this bad news? I will never forget that feeling. This was our son's firstborn. Everything was so new and exciting; then we got this bad report. I remember going and sitting in a chair in the waiting room. I put my face in my hands and asked God what was going on. I heard these words, "It's just warfare. Say 'no'!" So that's what I did. The whole family prayed. This was not to happen. Within 10 minutes, the nurse came out and told us that Haley's Apgar was up to 7 and that she would be fine. As I write this book, Haley is very alive and well, changing the world around her for Jesus.

Fear has a way of coming up and biting you. Everything seems to be going great in your life and you are walking in peace. All of a sudden, there fear is, trying to envelope you, trying to destroy your peace. We as believers have to make a choice to resist fear. We as a family had to make a choice that we would not partner with fear. The devil has legal rights only if we agree with him. The tool he uses to get us is fear. He does not play fair with us. He will go right for our soft spots.

> Do not be afraid of sudden fear, nor of the onslaught of the wicked when it comes; for the Lord will be your confidence and will keep your foot from being caught (Proverbs 3:25-26 NASB).

Do you ever just sit back and think about the world, what it looks like now, and what is really going on? Why are things in world events happening? What is really making those events happen? What is the root? Not just on the surface, but deeper—what is making things go the way they are going?

When I look at the world, I can recognize the devil's plan. The root is fear. It really is a simple plan. All the devil has to do is make sure that we walk in fear; then all of our responses will be out of that place of fear. The most repeated command in the Bible is "Do not fear." From Genesis to Revelation, God has repeatedly told us not to fear. God knows our humanness.

When I sit back and look at the world and see what God is doing, it makes me happy. Do these words sound familiar? "For I know the thoughts that I think toward you, says the Lord, thoughts of peace and not of evil, to give you a future and a hope" (Jer. 29:11).

Hitting the Mark

As intercessors, we need to be focused in our prayers and our strategies. Effective intercessors know how to listen for the plays that God calls, and they know how to catch the ball and make the touchdown. Effective intercessors are offensive intercessors; they know how to hit the mark.

My husband has a passion for hunting. He hunts all over the world. Every year we go to a hunting convention. They have room after room, equivalent to 12 football fields, full of everything you can think of that has to do with hunting. One of the things they do there is hold auctions. One year Bill bid on a hunt to South Africa and won. I had told him that I would go hunting with him if he took me somewhere warm. It's hard for me to understand hunters who go out and freeze just to bring home an animal. My dad and uncles all did it; my husband and my sons do it. I'm into warmth. Coldness and I don't get along very well. So I agreed that I would go hunting if he would take me to a warm climate. South Africa would be the place. It would be a hunting safari.

The first morning, we got up, (it was cold) we had breakfast, and instead of getting on down the road to hunt, we took a trip to the target range. You don't just get a gun and go out and shoot. The guide wants to make sure that, when you shoot an animal, your scope is on target so that you won't miss the animal or, worse yet, wound it. At the target range, you make sure that all the practice shots line up and that, when you shoot the bullet, it hits the mark. When we intercede, that's what we are doing; we are "hitting the mark."

One of the meanings for intercession is to "strike the mark." This phrase derives from the Hebrew word, *paga*.[1] *Paga* means "to meet"; it is the violent part of intercession. Job 36:32 tells of a violent *paga* meeting: "He covers His hands with lightning and commands it to strike [the mark]."

If we are going to be a people who pray with an offensive purpose, "hitting the mark" in our prayers, we must be on a quest to search the heart of God. How can we do that? Where do we go to find God's heart? We go to His Word to find His heart. I find it interesting that the word *Torah* comes from the root word *yarah*, which means "to shoot straight," or "to hit the mark."[2] God has given us the Bible to show us His heart.

In the late '90s, there was a real push for people to pray directly from the Scriptures. Praying the Scriptures is a great way to pray the heart of God. It's all there in writing, just waiting for us to pray and proclaim it. One of the main things that I learned during that season was how to meditate on the Scriptures. I learned how to take a chapter or a small section of Scripture and begin to think or meditate on it. I would read the verses over and over slowly. As I did, they began to go into my spirit. The Scriptures would become alive in my spirit and mind. Then, I would find myself praying from those verses. I would find new meaning and new revelation in each verse. My prayers would come alive. It felt as I prayed that I would hit the mark. There was focus in what I was praying. The Psalms are a great place to start to learn this method of prayer.

As I write this book, I am pondering a Psalm that I feel we need to hold on to and proclaim for this season.

A Joyful Return to Zion

A Song of Ascents.
When the Lord brought back the captivity of Zion,
We were like those who dream.
Then our mouth was filled with laughter,
And our tongue with singing.
Then they said among the nations,
"The Lord has done great things for them."
The Lord has done great things for us,
And we are glad.
Bring back our captivity, O Lord,
As the streams in the South.
Those who sow in tears
Shall reap in joy.
He who continually goes forth weeping,
Bearing seed for sowing,

Shall doubtless come again with rejoicing,
Bringing his sheaves with him (Psalm 126).

You can sit quietly and begin to read and think and get Holy Spirit understanding on this chapter. Begin to pray this chapter. Then stop and listen. You will get more understanding as you listen to the whisper of the Holy Spirit. He will tell you more. As He tells you more, begin to pray what He is telling you. In doing this, you are focused and you become targeted to the purpose of God. Your spirit and mind have become one with Heaven. You have become an offensive prayer warrior.

Paul was one person in the Bible who knew how to live an offensive lifestyle; Paul knew how to live from a place of victory. In First Corinthians 2:4-12,16, we can see that Paul knew that human reason is not a good Kingdom plan. Paul knew that not a lot of revival goes on with human wisdom. In fact, in First Corinthians 2, Paul says,

And my speech and my preaching were not with persuasive
words of human wisdom, but in demonstration of the Spirit
and of power, that your faith should not be in the wisdom of
men but in the power of God (1 Corinthians 2:4-5).

Paul was a very learned man and was more than able to use persuasive words of human wisdom to make his point. Instead, he chose to come in the Holy Spirit's power. Paul then went on to say that we don't even know the good things that God has prepared for those who love Him.

"Eye has not seen, nor ear heard, nor have entered into
the heart of man the things which God has prepared for

46

those who love Him." But God has revealed them to us through His Spirit. For the Spirit searches all things, yes, the deep things of God (1 Corinthians 2:9-10).

In these verses, Paul tells us that we can know the things of God because God has revealed them to us through His Spirit. Paul tells us that the Spirit is searching deeply into the heart of God. No one knows the heart of God except the Spirit. This is where it gets exciting. What we see in these Scriptures is that God is telling us that He has given us the ability to know the things of God. If we dive into the Spirit of God, we can know what is in the heart of God. Wow! God wants us to know Him and to know His ways.

A Spirit Fight

One of the targets that we have in our prayers and in all that we do at Bethel relates to our belief that God has promised us a cancer-free zone. That is one of our number one prayers. We are focused and determined to *hit the mark*. We know that we have the ball on this one. We have seen so many healed of this evil disease. We have also seen people die with this disease. But, we know that, as we continue to carry prayer down the field, we will hit the mark and reach the goal.

We know this is a spirit fight. One of the things that we are pushing against is a worldly mindset. I think of a worldly mindset as a humanistic, self-focused, carnal mindset that is not set on the things of God. The more we pray, read the Bible, preach, and "do" by healing the sick, the more we break down that mindset. Jesus did this very thing. He showed us how to spirit-fight. He broke down that worldly mindset by praying, preaching, and doing. One specific way that He broke down that mindset was by healing the sick. If someone you know does not believe that God heals, but witnesses a sick person being made whole after you lay your hands on them, this can break through the mindset of the unbelieving heart. We have seen that happen many times—where a person who didn't believe in healing became a believer after watching God heal someone.

And do not be conformed to this world, but be transformed by the renewing of your mind, that you may prove what is that good and acceptable and perfect will of God (Romans 12:2).

To me, this Scripture is a great example of a heavenly mindset. When our attention is fixed on Him, we are able to see His will more clearly. And when we think with a heavenly mindset, we begin to operate with an offensive lifestyle. You see, God has given us the ball, which is the Word of God, now it is our responsibility to pass it on to others.

Keep to the Plan

The sons of Issachar knew the signs of the times:

Of the sons of Issachar, men who understood the times, with knowledge of what Israel should do, their chiefs were two hundred; and all their kinsmen were at their command (1 Chronicles 12:32 NASB).

The part about this verse that I like is "with knowledge of what Israel should do." The sons had a plan. They not only understood the times, but they also knew what to do about the times in which they lived.

Jacob's blessing to Issachar was strength, rest between burdens, a pleasant land, and life as a burden-bearer (see Gen. 49:14-15). In the margin of my NKJV *Spirit-Filled Life Bible*, it says that Issachar was to be "basically docile, accepting a happy, quiet life in Canaan. They were politically insightful, switching allegiance from Saul to David."[3]

It sounds like the sons of Issachar didn't have a stressful life. They were just a happy people, enjoying their God-given land. I wonder if that's what made them so insightful into the comings and goings of the great nation of Israel. Their lives were free from worry and stress. They knew how to be happy.

At Bethel Church, my job is to oversee the prayer. As the Prayer Pastor, I get a lot of e-mails from all over the world. Many of the emails are asking for emergency prayer or have a high prayer alert. Many are good, but many are so full of fear that I must reject the spirit that is attached to them. I refuse to pray out of fear. What I *will* do is just stop and ask God how to pray about the crisis and for His direction. I stay focused on God and not on the crisis. When you move your prayers into fear, you can't possibly get a clear handle on how to pray according to how Heaven is praying. We must be like the sons of Issachar; we must understand and know what to do. Staying focused and keeping to the plan is most important.

The Old Testament is filled with great stories of kings and leaders of Israel who looked to God for wisdom. Their only hope and salvation was their dependence on what God would do. In

Second Kings 18–19 is the story of King Hezekiah and the great Assyria army. Assyria was located in what is now Iraq. The Assyrian nation, under the leadership of King Sennacherib, began moving south along the coast, attacking and taking city after city. Jerusalem was next on the list to be overthrown. In verse 35 of chapter 18, Sennacherib says,

> *Who among all the gods of the lands have delivered their countries from my hand, that the Lord should deliver Jerusalem from my hand?* (2 Kings 18:35).

Hezekiah tears his clothes, covers himself with sackcloth, and goes right into the house of the Lord (see 2 Kings 19:1). Now that's a good plan. Go right to the Presence. From there he sends a scribe, elders, and priests to the prophet Isaiah (see 2 Kings 19:2). Another good plan. Isaiah hears from God and sends the prophetic word back to the king:

> *Thus you shall say to your master, "Thus says the Lord: 'Do not be afraid of the words which you have heard, with which the servants of the king of Assyria have blasphemed Me.*
>
> *Surely I will send a spirit upon him, and he shall hear a rumor and return to his own land; and I will cause him to fall by the sword in his own land'"* (2 Kings 19:6-7).

King Sennacherib sends a letter filled with threats to King Hezekiah:

> *Thus you shall speak to Hezekiah king of Judah, saying: "Do not let your God in whom you trust deceive you, saying, 'Jerusalem shall not be given into the hand of the king of Assyria.'*

Look! You have heard what the kings of Assyria have done to all lands by utterly destroying them; and shall you be delivered?

Have the gods of the nations delivered those whom my fathers have destroyed, Gozan and Haran and Rezeph, and the people of Eden who were in Telassar?

Where is the king of Hamath, the king of Arpad, and the king of the city of Sepharvaim, Hena, and Ivah?" (2 Kings 19:10-13)

Now watch what happens next:

And Hezekiah received the letter from the hand of the messengers, and read it; and Hezekiah went up to the house of the Lord, and spread it before the Lord (2 Kings 19:14).

King Hezekiah does a prophetic act. He lays this threatening letter before the presence of God. He reminds God of who He is. It's not that God needs this reminder, but we need to agree with Heaven. This is a good place to start. He asked God to come through for his Jerusalem.

Now therefore, O Lord our God, I pray, save us from his hand, that all the kingdoms of the earth may know that You are the Lord God, You alone" (2 Kings 19:19).

Isaiah sends back to King Hezekiah and tells him that because he had prayed against Sennacherib of Assyria, God had heard him and would answer (see 2 Kings 19:20). That's a good day in Jerusalem!

What a great plan. One prophetic act brought forth an answer. It spoke into the invisible realm. This prophetic act came against a great demonic empire.

> *And it came to pass on a certain night that the angel of the Lord went out, and killed in the camp of the Assyrians one hundred and eighty-five thousand; and when people arose early in the morning, there were the corpses—all dead"* (2 Kings 19:35).

This story is a good example of living on the offensive. Hezekiah's plan "A" was God. He stayed focused on the ways of God. He understood the importance of being with God, in His presence.

It takes great courage to stay the course. You see this in Hezekiah. It will take great courage on our parts to stay the course when all around us things are falling apart.

Is your plan working for you? Is God your plan "A." Do you understand the importance of His presence and that being there will cause you to live an offensive lifestyle?

When we pray from the offensive lifestyle, our prayers are strong and mighty because we have spent so much time with God and He has stamped on our hearts who we are. Out of that relationship of love, we become strong love warriors, taking on the strategies from His heart. We know that, out of our love relationship with our Father, our prayers are mighty. Anything can happen.

God showed me several years ago just how strong our prayers are. In the late '90s, it was really cool to have a sword at church. Many of us felt like having a sword was saying prophetically that we were in a war and that God was fighting for us. We used them for spiritual warfare and making prophetic declarations. All kinds of prophetic acts were done using swords. I was in a conference where we called all the women up and knighted them for the Kingdom. It was a fun time.

I thought it would be really fun to get a dagger. I liked what daggers were used for in wartime. They used them to fight and to dig out arrow tips that had wounded them in battle.

I went onto a Website to order one. I found one called the state guardian dagger. Prophetically that sounded good to me. I felt like a guardian over my state. I ordered it and waited six long weeks for it to arrive. During this season in my life, I felt like I was going through a time of deafness in hearing God speak. It was a quiet time. Well, the day came when the dagger came to the house. I couldn't believe how big the box was. It must have been close to 6 feet high. I thought that they must really pack their goods well. As I unpacked the box, I reached in and began pulling out this very long sword. As I pulled the sword from the box, my spirit ears opened up and I heard, "You think your prayers are like a dagger, but I think your prayers are like this sword." The sword that I got in the mail that day was a two-handed claymore sword. William Wallace was said to have used this kind of sword as he fought for the freedom of Scotland. They were used in battle. Warriors used both their hands to hold the sword and would control their horses by their legs. There is a place on the sword that has a piece of leather wrapped around it for the second hand. Back in real wartime, they would take the skin of the enemy and wrap it around that part of the sword. Yeah, I know that's gross, but you get my point. This sword is called the *state guard.* When I called the company to tell them of the error, they told me to keep the sword.

I have never forgotten the word from the Lord that day. I felt like He pressed it on my heart with a personal gift.

On New Year's Eve day 2007, a group of us took that sword over to the Pacific coast to a little town where we have been praying for years. A demonically inspired spiritual leader of that region had passed on, and a lot of atmosphere shifting was going on. When a shift happens in the spirit realm, there seems to be confusion and crazy things go on. I just knew that, when this man died, there would be a shifting in the spirit realm leadership. Because we had been going there for years and partnering in prayer with the believers from that area, I felt the shift taking place a couple of weeks before this man died. When I got an email telling me he had died, the prophetic strategy for prayer all started coming together. Talking with others and finding out what they were feeling and hearing, we knew that it was important to go over before the New Year. We felt that there was a vying for demonic position. A week before all of this happened, I was at home watching two of my grandkids, Judah and Diego. We were playing upstairs in the guest room. Judah decided that he wanted to climb up the shelves in the closet and jump into a pile of blankets and pillows. Sounds like fun. I looked over at him while he was playing and heard the word, "Stabilize." As I listened more, I had a sense that God was speaking to me about the coming year—that 2008 would be a year of stabilization. The things that had been out of place would be brought back and stabilized. Not only that, but we as believers would also be the stabilizers. We would bring a stabilizing force where it was needed.

When we went over to the coast to pray, we realized that "stabilizing" was what we were doing that day—we were bringing a force of stability to the area and marking peace over the confusion. Bringing the sword and thrusting it into the sand on the beach was a prophetic act, showing the spirit realm that the prayers of the saints were powerful and mighty. Soon after this prayer trip, I talked with one of the pastors of that area. She told me that she was seeing more clearly, that she had more clarity and less confusion.

Our prayers are much bigger than we know. The strategies that God gives us to pray are world-changing!

The Power of One

The story of First Samuel chapter 14 is great! Many intercessors should be able to relate to this story. In reading and meditating on its content, one of the first things that I noticed was that verses 4 and 5 talk about two sharp rocks. Why would they even put this into the story? What does it have to do with anything? Why would the author describe what these rocks looked like and where they were?

> *Between the passes, by which Jonathan sought to go over to the Philistines' garrison, there was a sharp rock on one side and a sharp rock on the other side. And the name of one was Bozez, and the name of the other Seneh. The front of one faced northward opposite Michmash, and the other southward opposite Gibeah* (1 Samuel 14:4-5).

According to the *Spirit-Filled Bible*:

Bozez means "shining" or "slippery." *Senah* means "sharp craggy rock, thorny." It was the most improbable route one could choose, thus the surprise of the Philistines when Jonathan is discovered.[4]

To be in position in this spirit war is very important. Many times I have felt that we are going in stealth when we go into an area to pray. You may ask, "Is it important to go somewhere to pray, or can you just pray where you live?" Yes and yes. Most of the time, I have a very strong sense that it is important to go. Jonathan and his armor bearer didn't tell anyone because I'm sure that, if Jonathan had let everyone in on what he wanted to do, they would have tried to stop him, or they would have wanted to go with him. The latter would have defeated the whole plan. They would not have been able to go in secret. A lot of the time, our prayers as intercessors are done in secret. Then the prophetic acts that we go out and do are the fruit of our intercession.

King Saul was sitting under a pomegranate tree (see 1 Sam. 14:2). He did not want to take on the Philistines. Comfort was the name of his game. Israel was waiting and wanting their king to fight. Jonathan, seeing all this, had had it. So he with his armor bearer went secretly to take on the whole Philistines' camp (see 1 Sam. 14:6-14).

God is looking for intercessors who are passionate for Him and for His Kingdom to come. Whether by one or two is no matter to Him; it took one man who walked this planet over two thousand years ago to change the world forever. One man! Jesus.

Then Jonathan said to the young man who bore his armor, "Come, let us go over to the garrison of these uncircumcised; it may be that the Lord will work for us. For nothing restrains the Lord from saving by many or by few" (1 Sam. 14:6).

The NKJV *Spirit-Filled Bible*'s footnotes for First Samuel 14:6 read:

> The word *uncircumcised* was a term of derision often used by Israelites to designate Gentiles, or enemies. However, it is also a reminder of the covenant of God with His people. Jonathan and his armor bearer were covenant people of Yahweh; therefore, numerical odds do not apply, for the Lord was on their side.[5]

Don't you love Jonathan's courage and attitude? In saying this, he was making pronouncement over his enemies twofold: (1) you are the enemy of Yahweh, and (2) I carry a great multitude with me today. I am under a covenant with the God of all gods and the King of all kings.

That's the attitude we need in our spirits when we carry out our intercessions. Numbers have nothing to do with what God wants to do in the spirit realm. What matters is just passion and courage.

What Jonathan and his armor bearer did that day caused a great commotion, both in the invisible realm and the earthly realm. No one in his or her right mind would have done what Jonathan did that day, saying to his armor bearer,

> *Very well, let us cross over to these men, and we will show ourselves to them. If they say thus to us, "Wait until we come to you," then we will stand still in our place and not go up to them. But if they say thus, "Come up to us," then*

we will go up. For the Lord has delivered them into our hand, and this will be a sign to us (1 Samuel 14:8-10).

But, how many of us know that we don't fight this fight with our minds but with our spirits? Look what happens:

Then the men of the garrison called to Jonathan and his armor bearer, and said... "Come up to us, and we will show you something." Jonathan said to his armor bearer, "Come up after me, for the Lord has delivered them into the hand of Israel." And Jonathan climbed up on his hands and knees with his armor bearer after him; and they fell before Jonathan. And as he came after him, his armor bearer killed them. That first slaughter which Jonathan and his armor bearer made was about twenty men within about half an acre of land. And there was trembling in the camp, in the field, and among all the people. The garrison and the raiders also trembled; and the earth quaked, so that it was a very great trembling (1 Samuel 14:12-15).

Look at the fruit of one man's passion to see justice served:

Then Saul and all the people who were with him assembled, and they went to the battle; and indeed every man's sword was against his neighbor, and there was very great confusion. Moreover the Hebrews who were with the Philistines before that time, who went up with them into the camp from the surrounding country, they also joined the Israelites who were with Saul and Jonathan (1 Samuel 14:20-21).

The Hebrews and those who were in hiding, who were not a part of Saul's army—renegades—came to Saul's side to fight. The courage of one became the courage of many. When you look at Jonathan in this story, you can see how an offensive life is lived. You can see how nothing is impossible with God. As we carry out those seemingly crazy prophetic acts, choosing to live an offensive life before God, God will fight for us.

So the Lord saved Israel that day, and the battle shifted to Beth Aven (1 Samuel 14:23).

Let the shift begin.

ENDNOTES

1. Dutch Sheets, *Intercessory Prayer* (Ventura, CA: Regal Books, 1996), 50.

2. Allan Moorhead, "Law Verses Grace, Part 1" (2003), http://mayimhayim.org/Allen/Law%20vs%20Grace%201.htm (accessed 17 Sept 2008).

3. *Spirit-Filled Life Bible.* (Nashville: Thomas Nelson, Inc., Nelson Publishers, 1991), 77.

4. *Ibid.*, 413.

5. *Ibid.*

OWNERSHIP

I consider Redding, California, my home. Not only is it my home, it's my land. I believe that what I pray and speak over my city will make a difference. The same is true for you; where you live is yours. We are spiritual leaders in our land. As intercessors, we need to take that seriously.

Several years ago, there was a brutal murder in our city. Two young men murdered two other men just because they were homosexuals. I woke up that next morning and read the paper to hear that this had taken place in our county. I was saddened by the news. I went up to our prayer house and wept before God. I asked for forgiveness for the murders that we had committed in our city. I cried for mercy, that God would heal our land from the bloodshed.

Because you have plundered many nations, all the remnant of the people shall plunder you, because of men's blood and the violence of the land and the city…. "Woe to him who builds a town with bloodshed, who establishes a city by iniquity!" (Habakkuk 2:8,12)

You see, as an intercessor, it is my job to take ownership over what takes place in this area. You might say, "Wait a minute, you obviously didn't commit the crime, so why are you taking the blame?" Because I have taken "ownership" over my land, I take it personally when something takes place in this area that is sinful and wrong. If something has gone wrong, I see it as my responsibility to make it right through confession and repentance.

Many years ago, there was a multitude of First Nation people who were massacred in our area. At the time the massacre occurred, I wasn't even born. In fact, I had no part in this horrible atrocity. But, because God has placed me in this area, I believe that God has given me the responsibility to contend for this region. This region in Northern California is more than just my home; it is the place I love. As a result, I have become a reconciler, a person who prays for reconciliation, prays for healing to take place in the land. In fact, a reconciler helps to bring people together. *Reconciliation* means "to bring atonement; the act of harmonizing or making consistent; agreement of things seemingly opposite or inconsistent."[1]

Now all things are of God, who has reconciled us to Himself through Jesus Christ, and has given us the ministry of reconciliation, that is, that God was in Christ reconciling the world to Himself, not imputing their trespasses to

them, and has committed to us the word of reconciliation
(2 Corinthians 5:18-19).

In my repentance for this sin over a people and land, I was causing atonement to happen. We, through our intercession and repentance, bring harmony back into the atmosphere. Jesus took ownership over the sins that other people had committed, even though He was sin-free. When we take ownership over the sins that have taken place in a region and repent on behalf of those people, as if we were the very people who had committed those sins, we take ownership over the land.

One day while praying, I felt as if the Lord told me to pray for the government. The feeling was that it was a long-term prayer target, something I would pray for the rest of my life—so much so that my first email address had "prayfor5" in it. One of the meanings for the number *five* is the five-fold government. What kind of government did God want me to pray for? The three key areas are (1) physical government of our nation, (2) the spiritual government of our area and (3) the five-fold governmental offices of the Church—apostle, prophet, evangelists, pastor, and teacher.

At the time of the writing of this book, it has been 12 years, and the prayer subject has not changed. These are still three key areas in my life. These areas of prayer have led to some amazing adventures. God has brought many people with kindred spirits to help with this adventure. The strategies and prophetic acts that have transpired have been so fun and active and full of Holy Spirit energy.

I was reading a book on the history of the county we live in. As I read about the Indian massacres, I realized that something should be done. I began praying and asking God what we should do to bring about healing for our land? The Wintu Indians are the people group of the Redding area. They are the first landowners of this region. I have come to know several of them, and they are the most wonderful, giving people. Despite all of their wounds, they are a courageous people who continue to labor for their name. Many years ago, they lost their recognition and their name, and they still are not recognized by our government. There are many rules and regulations that they have to work through. It has been a hard struggle. But, they are a strong people.

God brought a wonderful Wintu Native American woman into my life named Donna. Or, should I say, I was brought into her life? We sat and talked and prayed together. She gave me information about her people. One day Donna came to me and asked if I had heard the saying, "Bury the hatchet." I said that I had. She told me that was what they did when they wanted to make things right, to end a dispute. We had just finished our prayer house but hadn't completed the landscape yet. We decided that we would "bury the hatchet" on the north side of the prayer house. That would be the perfect spot. We took a small group of people, and as a prophetic symbolic act, we buried the hatchet. Donna brought an Indian hatchet, and we buried it right in the ground. That was one of the first prophetic acts that we did together over our region. Donna, many other intercessors, and I have gone all over our county and prayed and released a cleansing atmosphere. In doing this, we as God's reconcilers are saying, "God, we know that you have given us the responsibility to bring about the ministry of reconciliation, and we are taking ownership of that. We will do all that you want us to do, when you want us to do it, and you will show us how to do it."

I attended a conference here in Redding years ago. They had a guest speaker who was a First Nations leader. As he was speaking about helping the First Nations peoples, he mentioned helping out monetarily. I realized that we needed to put our money where our mouth was. We had somewhat of a relationship with the Wintu people through our friend Donna, but that was all. One of our elders in our church was at the conference as well. He emailed us and mentioned that he had heard this same thing at the meeting and thought that it would be a great idea to give to the Wintu tribe. I called our friend and asked if Bill and I could meet with the Tribal Council. So she made the arrangements. Meanwhile, we arranged a letter to give to the Wintu Tribe along with a check. In the letter, we addressed them as being the first landowners of this area and honored them for who they are. We also explained that Bethel Church, our church, would be giving them a check every month as long as Bethel was around.

That night at the tribal meeting, there wasn't a dry eye in the place. It was a moment I will never forget. The reconciliation that went on in all of our hearts forever changed the atmosphere of our city. Yes, there are still wounds and hurts, but we have friends now, and we continue to pray and help when we are asked. That night at the meeting, many gifts were exchanged. One was a tree that we received from the tribe, a red bud tree. We planted it at our prayer house garden. Since that time, we have received other trees from the tribe as a confirmation of our relationship.

Soon after this gathering, we began seeing the issues of the First Nations peoples being brought up in the news. We saw that there were still struggles but that recognition was beginning to surface. Honor was being given to whom it was due (see Rom. 13:7).

There are many examples in the Bible of intercessors—the greatest being Jesus. When Jesus said, "It is finished," (John 19:30) that was the end of His intercession here on earth. Remember, an intercessor pleads with somebody in authority on behalf of somebody else, especially someone who is to be punished. Jesus was our intercession. He stood between God and human sin. Not only did He stand on our behalf, but He also became sin.

For He made Him who knew no sin to be sin for us, that we might become the righteousness of God in Him (2 Corinthians 5:21).

For what the law could not do in that it was weak through the flesh, God did by sending His own Son in the likeness of sinful flesh, on account of sin: He condemned sin in the flesh...(Romans 8:3).

Another time I will never forget is when our city dedicated our new Sundial Bridge, July 4, 2004. First thing, the city asked the Wintu Tribal Chief to come and be the first on the bridge and to pray over it. So as a whole large crowd of people watched on one side of the bridge, the Tribal Chief and a delegate of the Tribal Council walked across from the other side. I had never heard of anything like this honoring of the tribe happening in Redding before. As our city watched the ceremony, some of us cried because we knew that the reconciliation that had gone on in that council meeting had caused a domino effect in our city. As the Tribal Council finished its part of the ceremony, the chief's mother, who was standing by her son, turned to me and mouthed a "thank you." We both knew why.

That's ownership—taking your place as an owner who bears responsibility. In a business, the owner does whatever he or she must do to keep that business in favor with the community. Well, as intercessors we do the same. We do whatever we need to do to keep our region in favor with God. When we repent on behalf of people who have committed sins in the land, we call this *identificational repentance*.

In Shasta County, there is a two-and-a-half-month harvest season for marijuana. Because a lot of Shasta County is remote and in the foothills of the north end of the state of California, there is quite a lot of marijuana grown, not just in our county, but also in the counties all around us. It is a big business. The money that is brought in from the growth of marijuana is, in turn, used to make other drugs. When I was a teacher's aide many years ago, all of the teachers had to take a drug abuse awareness and prevention education class. They told us that marijuana was the gateway drug, that when you start using marijuana, it was only a matter of time before you experimented with other drugs. It is also the drug that gives you the money to buy more dangerous drugs.

One of the women in our church told me that one of her sons wanted to talk to me about the drug business in our area. This young man was not saved and was a drug runner himself. I agreed to meet with him and talk. He began to tell me many interesting things about our area and what was going on. It was very informative and gave me some insight that stirred me up for prayer. I asked God to show me how to pray with a strategy.

I like watching the Weather Channel, and I also like to read the weather page in our local newspaper. My husband doesn't understand why I would sit and watch the Weather Channel. I think it must be that the weather is foretelling. It lets you know what is coming. I had been praying about this whole drug ring in our community for about two weeks. One morning I was reading the weather page of our newspaper and noticed a little box with the new moon phases. I had never paid attention to that before, but it caught my eye that morning. That little box showed me the date and times of the full moon and new moon. I mentally put that information into my head and finished reading the paper. When I was done, I picked up my Bible and began reading where I had left off: Psalm 81. I read through verse 4 and stopped. It read:

Blow the trumpet at the new moon, at the full moon, on our feast day. For it is a statute for Israel, an ordinance of the God of Jacob (Psalm 81:3-4 NASB).

So something stopped me, and I realized that it wasn't a mistake that I had just read about the moon phases in the newspaper and then read about it in the Bible. Sitting there, I knew instantly what I would do. In that moment, I knew what God was telling me to do. It's called the language of the Spirit. It's your spirit man picking up on the movement of Heaven. I felt that I was to go to the north border of our state and blow the shofar at the moon phase at sunrise. We have learned through experience that, when praying at sunrise, there is an open Heaven. It feels like a straight shot right from Heaven to earth. One of my friends met a Native American spiritual leader who looked at her and said, "Oh, you pray early in the morning, don't you?" She responded, "Yes, I do." He told her that, when you pray at sunrise, there is an openness.

So having this information, I called a friend, told her what was going on, and asked if she would go with me. We waited until the next moon phase then headed up to the border. We got there right at sunrise and blew that shofar. When we got back into the car, we began to pray. Out of my mouth came these word, "Lord, I ask that you forgive us for allowing a sorcery spirit to come into our region." Deep intercession came on us as we cried for our state, asking God to redeem us and have mercy. As always, we ended in a time of joy and praise. Then we drove home.

That time happened to be the harvest time for marijuana crops. A week went by. One day, looking at the paper, I saw our first answer: a drug bust had happened. So for the next two and a half months, we watched daily more and more "good" harvesting. Not only that, there were several other kinds of drug busts. There was a U-Haul truck traveling on Interstate 5 just south of us. It got in a wreck, tipped over, and spilled out a methamphetamine lab. Another time a man was pulled over by a highway patrolman for doing an illegal lane change, nothing to be arrested for, but another patrolman pulled up, and he had a dog in his car. The dog was trained in smelling drugs. They opened the man's trunk and found 1.1 million worth of cocaine. This man was on his way to Canada. By the end of the harvest season, the paper reported that it had been the biggest police harvest of marijuana in the history of Shasta County. I got a call from the young man who gave me all the information. He told me that one of his friends in Canada called him wondering what was going on because there were hardly any drugs coming through.

I have to tell you that, when this young man walked out of the office that day, I told him that he would soon find out who he was. Within two weeks, he came to the Lord and was saved. Eventually, he graduated from our ministry school. Wow! It was a very exciting season of answered prayers rising from one big strategy that worked.

One of the ministries here in our city has done a great job in bringing city leaders and spiritual city leaders together. We meet from time to time to have lunch and talk. At one of these meetings, our sheriff was asked to share about what is happening in our city. Not everything he talked about was good news that day. But it was good to hear so that we would pray more effectively as spiritual leaders. One good thing he talked about was the way that the police department has been working to fight against the drug problem in our city. He told us that they had just completed an operation to harvest marijuana plants. In two weeks, they had harvested 284,000 plants, and by the season's end they were projecting 365,000 plants. Five thousand plants bring in $1.6 billion.

I want to go back a little in this story and talk about the prayer that we prayed up on the border: "Forgive us for allowing a sorcery spirit into our region." There are three verses in the Bible that talk about sorcery: Second Chronicles 33:6, Galatians 5:20, and Revelation 18:23. In Second Chronicles 33:6, the word *sorcery* is the Hebrew word, *kashaph*, meaning "to practice witchcraft or sorcery, sorcerer, sorceress."[2] In the next two verses from Galatians and Revelation, the word *sorcery* is a Greek word, *farmakeia (pharmakeia)*, meaning "the use or the administering of drugs, poisoning, sorcery, magical arts."[3] When we prayed that day up on the border, we were right on track. Once again we were taking ownership. We were asking for a cleansing to happen over the land.

This makes so much sense and gives us understanding into the life of drug addiction. It is like a spell. As we pray over those we love who are addicted and caught in that curse of the devil, let's remember to address the sorcery that has come to destroy them. Let us be the go-between for those we know who are living in addictions.

One of my favorite stories on taking ownership in the Bible is in Genesis 26.

There is a famine in the land and Isaac is on his way to Egypt. Along the way, he stops in Gerar. God speaks to him and tells him to stay there and not go down to Egypt. In verse 2, God tells him to live in the land in which "I tell you" (see Gen. 26:2). God says in verses 3-5 that He wants Isaac to dwell in this land, that He will bless Isaac and his descendants:

> *Dwell in this land, and I will be with you and bless you; for to you and your descendants I give all these lands, and I will perform the oath, which I swore to Abraham your father. And I will make your descendants multiply as the stars of heaven; I will give to your descendants all these lands; and in your seed all the nations of the earth shall be blessed; because Abraham obeyed My voice and kept My charge, My commandments, My statutes, and My laws* (Genesis 26:3-5).

So, verse 6 says that Isaac dwells in the land as God commands him to do, and verse 12 says that Isaac sowed in the land (see Gen. 26:6,12). But in verses 7-11, Issac lies to Abimelech, saying that Rebekah is his sister rather than his wife. Have you ever wondered, like me, why verses 7-11 were put in the Bible? I'm sure there are many reasons those verses are in there. Maybe it's because his father Abraham did the same thing and there is a lesson to be learned. Or, maybe it's just that God covers us when we do stupid things. That little lie of Isaac could have caused the death of someone. Who knows maybe even a war. But God. It's always *but God*.

> *But God, being rich in mercy, because of His great love with which He loved us* (Ephesians 2:4 NASB).

I really like these parts of the Bible that show the human side of humankind, that show how much we need God's mercy every minute. As we continue on with this story of Isaac, we understand that Isaac is dwelling and sowing in the land. When God tells Isaac to dwell in the land, God is saying to Isaac, "I want you to stay for a long time. This is your land." For that is what *dwell* means: "to live as a resident."[4] So that is what Isaac did. Isaac also sowed the land. That means he was a farmer. It says that Isaac sowed in that land and reaped in the same year a hundred-fold, and the Lord blessed him. The Bible says that Isaac was so blessed and so prosperous that the Philistines who lived there envied him. The king even asked them to move away from them.

In Genesis 21:22-34, Abraham had dug a well and King Abimelech's servant had seized the well. Because of this seizure, the king asked Abraham to be kind to him and not hurt him or his people. Upon agreement to this, the two men made a covenant together. The agreement was that the well belonged to Abraham, that this well would be called *Beersheba* (the oath). (See Genesis 21:22-34.)

Now, you might be wondering what is so important about a well. If you have ever been to Israel and traveled to the southern part where Beersheba is, you know how important water is. It is very dry there, but it wasn't only that. Anytime anyone dug a well, he or she was claiming that land surrounding the well. So, when Abraham dug the well of Beersheba, he was saying, "This is my land and my descendants' land."

Verse 15 of Genesis 26 tells us that the Philistines had stopped up all the wells that Abraham had dug (see Gen. 26:15). What they were doing—and I believe they knew exactly what they were doing—was hiding any evidence that the land belonged to anyone else. In researching this verse, I found that not only did they fill the wells up with dirt, but they also put dead animals in the wells and made it look like nothing had ever been there. It's interesting that the very thing that was used to make the covenant was the thing used to try to break the covenant.

I think that, while Isaac was sowing the land, he discovered his father's wells. The Bible says that he re-dug all of his father's wells and gave them back their names (see Gen. 26:18). Isaac came into the land, found what was his, and took ownership once again. The story goes on to say that he dug five more wells in that region, that the king came back to him and said, "We have certainly seen that the Lord is with you. Let there now be an oath between us" (Gen. 26:28). Isaac only took back what was rightfully his.

When we pray over our land and re-dig wells—these things that were once places of life—and find new wells of living water, we are doing just what Isaac did. He reclaimed his land; we reclaim our land. Then God will favor us and all will see that favor over us and the land that God has given.

ENDNOTES

1. *The New Webster Encyclopedic Dictionary of the English Language*, s.v. "Reconciliation."

2. "The Old Testament Hebrew Lexicon," *Studylight.org*, s.v. "Kashaph," http://www.studylight.org/lex/heb/view.cgi?number=3784 (accessed 19 Sept 2008).

3. "The NAS New Testament Greek Lexicon," *Crosswalk.com*, s.v. "Farmakeia/Pharmakeia," http://www.bible studytools.net/Lexicons/Greek/ grk.cgi?number=5331 &version=nas (accessed 19 Sept 2008).

4. *Merriam-Webster's Collegiate Dictionary*, s.v. "Dwell."

5

JESUS, OUR EXAMPLE OF JOY

We pastored the church in Weaverville, California, as I mentioned previously, for 17 years. It was a joy for us to raise three lively children in a small mountain community. The church was a family. For several years, whenever Easter would come around, we would have Easter sunrise service and then go to different homes for an Easter breakfast. Especially to our second son, Brian, who at the time was around three years old, food was very special. He loved those special times because there were sweet foods, too.

We were sitting at the table eating our Easter breakfast, but Brian was having a hard time eating his eggs because he had spotted the cinnamon rolls over on the stove. Reasoning with him just wasn't working, so Bill, being a man full of wisdom, picked

Brian up with his plate of eggs, walked over to the stove, and said, "Brian if you eat your eggs, you can have a cinnamon roll." So Brian sat there in Bill's arms eating his eggs, all the time staring at the cinnamon rolls. When he finished, he got his roll. He had endured the cross (eggs) for the joy (roll) set before him. This may be a silly story, but it does illustrate a good point.

Intercessors should be the happiest people on the planet because they know the plans of God. God is in a good mood, and He wants to give good gifts to His children. As intercessors, our job is to look ahead to the good gifts that God wants to give to us and to agree with those plans. As intercessors, we have to be OK with the fact that God is OK with *motivating* us with gifts. We can see this in the Scriptures.

> *Looking unto Jesus, the author and finisher of our faith, who for the joy that was set before Him endured the cross, despising the shame, and has sat down at the right hand of the throne of God* (Hebrews 12:2).

Jesus endured so much while He was here on earth, and He endured it for the *promise of joy* that was set before Him. Jesus is into *joy!* We see here that the King of kings and Lord of lords became a man, which was His choosing. And He endured it all for joy. That, in itself, was enough to give Him all of the endurance He needed—enduring the suffering of just being in a man's body after living in the heavenly realm full of light, power, and joy! In my opinion, the joy is what kept Him enduring the earthly living and the dying.

We have an elementary school at our church in Redding. Every year they have a program in the form of dance and drama.

It's about creation, the life of Jesus, and the war between the demonic realm and angelic realm. One of the scenes shows the angels standing in Heaven watching as Jesus is being accused, beaten, and eventually crucified on the cross. The angels are so disturbed because they have been given instructions not to come to His defense. At no other time had they been prevented from helping Jesus. The Scriptures say He endured this because of the joy.

We believe, as a people of God's power, that we are to bring Heaven to earth. Joy is a very big part of Heaven. Heaven is filled with joy. It is our responsibility to bring that here on earth.

There is no depression in Heaven, so we have no legal right to depression. If you are depressed, you need to recheck your life. Figure out why, and for Heaven and earth's sake, take care of it. The world needs to see happy, joyful, alive people of God who love and serve out of joy.

If I say, "I will forget my complaint, I will put off my sad face and wear a smile" (Job 9:27).

You might be thinking, "But what about all the horrible stuff that is going on in the world? Shouldn't that affect us?" Yes, it should. I met with a woman in our church who wanted to let me know some things that were going on in our city with the occult. After we met, I headed right over to our prayer house. I was feeling a little weighty and needed to get God's perception on all that I had heard. As I walked in the prayer garden, I had a vision. In the vision, I was in a familiar place with Jesus. We were walking and holding hands, similar to the way that two best girlfriends would hold hands, shoulder to shoulder. It felt like we were sharing intimate secrets. I was talking to Him about the information I had just received. I looked over at His other hand, which was closed. I could tell that He was holding something in secret in that hand. I asked Him what He had in His hand. He opened His hand, and I saw that He was holding the whole world. It looked so small. When I saw that, all of the heaviness left, and I realized that He has everything under His control and in His hand. Now, that doesn't mean that I don't continue to pray over these matters for my city. But it does mean that I can't carry the heaviness. See, Jesus already did that. He carried it all to the cross.

What comes with Jesus' completeness on the cross is that we can now fight *from* victory not *for* victory. We as intercessors are praying and begging God for things that are already ours because of what Jesus did on the cross. When Jesus said, "It is finished," can you imagine what happened in all of Heaven and on earth? I can see the demonic realm saying, "Yeah, it's finished and we won," only to be shocked in three days when Jesus overcame death. Yes, it was finished for the demons of hell. They had to go back to the drawing board and form a whole new plan. But in Heaven, they knew what Jesus was saying. All was complete now—all that Jesus had set out to accomplish on earth, including being that living example to us. He was done.

It's very important that, as intercessors, we have a revelation of what Jesus did while He was here on the earth. Jesus came to set the captive free. He healed the sick, raised the dead, and cast out demons (see Luke 4:18). If we continually carry around an attitude of sorrows, lugging around what Jesus already carried to the cross (all of the sins and feelings that go with that sorrow), then we are denying what Jesus did for all mankind. Did you notice that I said, "carry"? I'm speaking to those who "carry" the weight and heaviness of another person around even though Jesus already carried it to the cross for us. Jesus said, "It is finished!" My husband has a sermon message with this statement, "What part of finished don't you understand?" If we can catch this thought and put it into our hearts, our prayer lives will change. We will become confident in what Jesus did, and we will become releasers of His Kingdom here on earth.

I'm not saying that there aren't times during deep prayer that we feel and pray with a burden. We can carry this in times of prayer, but I feel that we are not allowed to carry it outside of our intercessions. There is an exchange program for us. We give him *weary heavy burdens*; He gives us *rest*.

I've noticed that people with a mercy gift seem to struggle with carrying this heaviness more than others. They need to see mercy and justice done, and when it is not, they can carry around the hurt and wounds. You can see it in their eyes. It becomes *unsanctified mercy* because it is carried in human strength. The best solution is to press into God more and to receive His words. When I saw that little world in Jesus' hand, it took all of my fear and worry away.

The Fear Factor

Fear is our enemy. You can pretty much find fear wrapped around any issue in your life that is not centered on the things of the Kingdom. A note about familiar spirits: they are familiar, and at times they are the only things that can falsely comfort us. Therefore, we can feel good in a warped kind of way.

When you have a radical encounter with God, you now have the tools to fight back. In the church in Weaverville, my husband led a Friday night prayer meeting. One time, I came late to the meeting. I felt really under it and depressed. We were going through a really big change in our ministry, and I had opened the door to a familiar spirit. I should have known better. I thought that I could feel just a little sorry for myself. That was my mistake. I came into the room and walked right over to where Bill was. He was at the keyboard leading the worship time. I sat right at his feet. He told me later that when I sat down, he looked down at me, and on my leg was a little demon. He reached down to brush it away and it bit him as it left.

Wild, but I believe that demon was a familiar spirit sent to torment me. I understood something that night. As God gives you freedom, it is your responsibility to keep it. You can't go opening up old feelings and old thought patterns that you walked in under bondage. When you do that, you give permission for the tormenter to come. I did get free that night, thanks to my husband's discernment. This is what Second Corinthians 10:3-5 is talking about when it says:

> *For though we walk in the flesh, we do not war according to the flesh. For the weapons of our warfare are not carnal but mighty in God for pulling down strongholds, casting down arguments and every high thing that exalts itself against the knowledge of God, bringing every thought into captivity to the obedience of Christ.*

The Joy of Jesus

There is much suffering in this world. Jesus suffered. But Jesus knew where His strength was. He had experienced great joy in Heaven. All of Heaven is joy. The Bible says that we will enter into the joy of the Lord one day (see Matt. 25:21). While Jesus lived on this earth, I believe that He knew how to live out of joy, even in the midst of suffering. Remember, Jesus is our perfect example of how to live here on earth. In the movie, *The Passion*, there is a scene where Jesus is at His home building a table. His mother comes out, and they are laughing together. That's one of my favorite parts of the movie. I know it's something the writer added to the movie, but I can imagine that that is how Jesus lived. I believe Jesus laughed a lot and enjoyed life. He was able to bring the joy of Heaven to earth.

If we feed ourselves on life and joy and what God is doing here on earth, we will live like Jesus lived on earth. But, if we feed ourselves on bad news all of the time, if that is our focus in life, then we will live out of fear and despair.

Stories of Joy

I like to imagine. God has given us a wonderful tool: our imaginations. When I read the stories in the Bible, I use my imagination to look at the whole story. What do you see when you read about Jesus healing the sick? Do you see that He healed the sick, or can you see the joy all around Him as He healed? I know that when we pray for the sick and they get healed, there is a lot of joy around. Everyone is happy. Some get so excited that you will see dancing and celebration. I don't think that it was any different for Jesus and His disciples. When the eyes of the blind were opened and the person who had been deaf all his life could hear for the first time, there was joy and excitement. This is where we need to live. We are releasers of Heaven and all that Heaven holds.

Do you think that when Jesus released life over the little girl in Mark 5:38-42 that there wasn't joy? You can see joy released as you read this story from *The Message Bible*:

> *They entered the leader's house and pushed their way through the gossips looking for a story and neighbors bringing in casseroles.*
>
> *Jesus was abrupt: "Why all this busybody grief and gossip? This child isn't dead; she's sleeping."*
>
> *Provoked to sarcasm, they told him he didn't know what he was talking about. But when He had sent them all out, He took the child's father and mother, along with His companions, and entered the child's room.*
>
> *He clasped the girl's hand and said, "Talitha koum," which means, "Little girl, get up."*
>
> *At that, she was up and walking around! This girl was twelve years of age. They, of course, were all beside themselves with joy* (Mark 5:38-42 TM).

Don't you love that? They, of course, were all "beside themselves with joy" (Mark 5:42 TM). That's the real life of Christ. He brought Heaven to earth, and Heaven is filled to overflowing with great joy. Heaven is just waiting to pour it out on us.

In John 10:10, Jesus says, "The thief comes to steal, kill and destroy. I have come to give life and life more abundantly." Then, in First John 3:8, it says, "The Son of God appeared for this purpose, to destroy the works of the devil" (NASB).

That should make us all jump up and down with joy. But, it gets better.

In Matthew 28:18-19, there is a transfer of authority to us! Jesus says:

> *All authority has been given to Me in heaven and on earth.* **Go** *therefore and make disciples of all the nations, baptizing them in the name of the Father, and of the Son and of the Holy Spirit* (Matthew 28:18-19).

He is handing His authority over to us to *go*. Go do the stuff that He is telling us to do. In Matthew 10:8, He tells us to "Bring health to the sick. Raise the dead. Touch the untouchables. Kick out the demons. You have been treated generously, so live generously" (TM).

Moments of Joy

Talk about a life of joy. When we travel to different parts of the world, we have the joy of praying for hundreds of people. One of the things that I like the most is seeing people hear that God is in a good mood and that He wants to bless them. When they understand that, they have authority to do the stuff that Jesus did, and they begin to use their authority for the first time. Watching them pray for the sick and see someone healed under their hand for the first time is incredible! There in that moment is much joy.

We were in Mexico doing a healing crusade. It was at the end of the meeting, and Bill had called our team up to pray for the sick. We had brought a team with us from home. One of the guys on the team had never prayed for the sick before. The first person that came up to him was deaf in one ear. As he began to pray, the person was completely healed. Everyone was excited, including the team member who had prayed for him to be healed. Word got out in the meeting that he was the one to go to for prayer if you were deaf. So he had a line of people. Everyone, with the exception of one, who stood in his line was healed that night. A lot of happy people went home that night. Healing and joy were released, and the works of the devil were destroyed. Yeah God!

God wants to release joy to us. Joy is the pulse of Heaven; let's bring it here to earth.

THE THREE REALMS

When I began this journey into intercession, I didn't say, "OK I'm going to be an intercessor now." Instead, I simply fell into the third realm of Heaven, and I fell madly in love with the Holy Spirit. I touched a realm that I had never experienced before. I am now so very addicted to His presence; His realm is where I always want to dwell.

One of the things that we have felt, in all of our travels, is the importance of carrying His joy wherever we go. That is our assignment from Heaven. Remember there is great joy in Heaven, and that is our model for life and ministry here on earth.

But to the Son He says: "Your throne, O God, is forever and ever; a scepter of righteousness is the scepter of Your kingdom. You have loved righteousness and hated law-lessness; therefore God, Your God, has anointed You with the oil of gladness more than Your companions" (Hebrews 1:8-9).

God is speaking about His Son, Jesus, and because He had loved righteousness and hated lawlessness, God has given Him the oil of gladness. He had more joy than all of His brethren. He even endured the cross because of the joy set before Him. This tells us that joy is one of Heaven's greatest treasures. God has anointed Jesus with gladness. That word *gladness* is "exuberant joy." That is what our Jesus is anointed with: exuberant joy. We know that Jesus is our example. Therefore, we should carry that same anointing. *Anointing* means, in the Hebrew Dictionary, "to smear." In the New World Dictionary, the word *anoint* means to rub oil or ointment on. Anointing, that exuberant joy that was poured over Jesus, is what He carried upon Himself.

When we hang around in the presence of Jesus, we will come into contact with that joy. Have you noticed that a couple who has been married a long time begins to look like each other? And, they can even act like each other. The more we spend time with Jesus, the more we will become like Him. You want more joy? Do what that psalmist did in Psalm 73. He went before God. He poured out his heart to God; he found God's presence. We need to go before God and stay there until we feel Him and are changed.

I have some friends who are wild and crazy and love traveling around the world to pray. Our very first trip together was to Alaska. I had been praying one day, and the subject of prayer was Alaska. When the Holy Spirit downloads new ideas, I make it a habit to begin to meditate and pray over these things. Alaska was one of those things. I happened to mention it to one of my wild friends one day, and she said that the very same thing was going on with her. Obviously, we knew that we needed to pursue this thought. We began studying and getting insight on why we were praying. We decided that we were to go to Alaska.

The next decision was where we should go. When you get a strategy from Heaven, it's a funny thing; you start getting all kinds of confirmation. A young man in our church came to me during this time with a dream. After he had the dream, he felt he was to tell me. He did not know that we were planning a prayer trip to Alaska. In the dream, he was leading a group of people upward. There was an angel guide with him. They got to a second plain and decided to stay there because it was so nice. The guide told him not to stay in that place but to go higher. The name of that second plain was Shinar. As he woke up, a Scripture came to him: Genesis chapter 11. Genesis 11 is the account of the Tower of Babel. Verse 2 says, "And it came to pass, as they journeyed from the east, that they found a plain in the land of Shinar, and they dwelt there" (Gen. 11:2). Shinar is Babylon. For centuries it was considered the most fertile place on the earth. When this young man gave me that dream, I knew that it was a dream to pay attention to.

I had read a great book by George Otis Jr., *The Twilight Labyrinth*.[1] I enjoy reading history. This book takes you way back to the beginning. With this dream and that book, I began to get some good insight on the plan for our trip. In the book, George Otis Jr. talks about the migration of the people groups. In Genesis 11:6-8, the Trinity is speaking and Jesus says,

Indeed, the people are one, and they all have one language, and this is what they begin to do; now nothing that they propose to do will be withheld from them. Come, let Us go down and there and confuse their language, that they may not understand one another's speech. So the Lord scattered them abroad from there over the face of all the earth, and they ceased building the city.

God came down to confuse the languages of the people.

God's people had slowly rebelled and moved away from the heavenly presence and relationship that their ancestors had experienced. They had lost God. In Genesis 11:4, they took it upon themselves to make a name for themselves. Francis Schaeffer calls this "the first declaration of humanism."[2] It was not just the building of a tower; it was the attitude behind it.

When God came down and confused their language, a great migration began to all parts of the world. On one of the migration paths were the people who came to Alaska through the Bering Land Bridge. An important focal point for us was what they brought with them: the practice of Shamanism, a religion of northern Asia in which shamans can intercede between humanity and powerful evil spirits.

Praying at Heaven's Gates

We decided to go through the Bering Land Bridge because of what had been brought through there spiritually. We decided to go to Nome, Alaska, to the gate between Russia and Alaska. We felt that, when we went, God would bring healing and redemption to the land and open a gate. It took two years before *eight* of us (the number for new beginnings) took off for Alaska. Eight women going to Alaska can stir up quite the conversation. Because we had such an early flight out of Anchorage to Nome that morning, we decided to sleep in the airport. What a sight. (Never sleep on the floor of an airport, especially in Alaska. Very cold.) As we boarded the plane that morning, the stewardess asked us what eight women were doing going to Nome. Men go to Alaska to hunt; that makes sense. But eight women, and especially to Nome? Nome is known for one thing. It's the finish line for the Iditarod Trail Sled Dog Race. There is nothing there. So we told her that we were going there to pray and to open a spiritual gate. She became so excited about this information. She told us that she had done the same thing. Two weeks before, she had taken a team to Barrow, Alaska, and in the spirit opened a gate there. (I believe that there are spiritual gates in the heavenlies that need to be opened to give more access to the heavenly realm of God. You can also call these gates, *portals*. I believe that when you access these gates or portals, you are opening a place for more of Heaven to come in that region.) When we heard this, we got excited with her.

Here's where the story really gets exciting. When she was able to talk to us again, she asked us where we were from. We told her that we were from California. She got excited again. A year before, she had received a prophetic word that a team would be coming from California and that, when they came, they would open a gate in the spirit realm. Well, we all got really excited. We all knew by now that we were really on to something.

The Blessing in Nome

We landed in Nome and went to the hotel. We felt that we were to pray in our room first and then go out on the street to pray. As intercessors, we get pretty excited in our prayers, and we make a lot of noise at times. This was no exception. We had an awesome time of releasing and prophesying over the region. We saw an eagle coming up and going out over the land. One of the girls stood in the middle of the room and began to pray in tongues. The tongue sounded like an Indian dialect. It was intense and amazing. We ended our time in holy laughter. That was a new experience for us. I still think to this day that laughter was the most effective thing that we did all day. Just as we were ending our time, a knock came at the door. We thought maybe they were going to kick us out of the hotel for making so much noise. One of the girls answered the door. There stood three maids that I think were the only maids in the hotel. They were holding a basket of soaps and shampoos that we hadn't asked for. They were there because they wanted to thank us for coming to pray in Nome. They told us that no one had ever come there to pray before. That would have been worth the whole trip for us—just to go and bless people and places, just to bring a small town into its destiny. What excitement to partner with Heaven and bring blessings.

After praying at the hotel, we moved out to the street and began walking. I had brought an old key. We like to deposit keys wherever we go as a symbolic prophetic act of freedom. So we threw this one in the Bering Strait Sea to release the native people of the land to freedom. As we were walking past a bar, a couple came out. We began talking to them and found out that the lady was sick. We were able to pray for her, and she was really ministered to. One of the Native American friends from home had given me some handmade jewelry to give away as gifts. I gave this lady on the street a necklace and told her that it was from another

Native American from our home. What fun that was. We then met a young lady on the main street. She was the only one walking on the street. We asked her if she would take our picture. She asked us what we were all doing in Nome. We told her why we had come, and she said, "Would you come to my house? I moved here a year ago and have been praying for all of Alaska." Another divine appointment. We went to her home. She pulled out maps and papers. We lay on the floor with her and prayed over Alaska. It was glorious. We ended up spending two hours with her. Wow!

The next morning we got up early and left Nome. The same stewardess was on our plane. When she saw us, she was so relieved. She told us that she had been praying for us and that we needed to get on this flight because it was the only one going out of Nome for the next several days. There was a big storm coming in, and it would have stranded us for days.

A couple days after this trip, one of the women called me and told me that she had been looking online for any news about Nome. The Nome paper was reporting that the only female federal judge was coming to Nome to talk about the Native Americans and how the judicial system could help with their issues. The article also said that Nome would be her eighth stop. She planned on going to 20 different stops in Alaska. Our trip to Alaska was counted as a success and will always be a memorable experience. As our first prayer trip, it was a hallmark to jumpstart our around-the-world prayer experiences. Since then, we have gone to many places to pray like that.

The Realms

Intercessors have the ability to pick up many things that are going on in the spirit realm. Often, it seems like intercessors get so focused on what the devil is doing that they don't look at what God is doing. The question is not, *What is the devil doing*. The question should be, *What is God doing?* This should be the life theme of all of the people of God. But, here's the deal. There are times when intercessors can pick things up from the demonic realm. And some intercessors will get stuck here and even live out of this place. They begin living out of the first and second realms.

Let me explain. There are three "realms" that are mentioned in the Bible. The word *realm* means a region, sphere, or area.[3] The Bible specifically talks about the first realm, the second realm, and the third realm. The first realm is the realm that you can see with your eyes. It's the physical realm. "Now I saw a new heaven and a new earth, for the *first heaven* and the *first earth* had passed away. Also there was no more sea" (Rev. 21:1). So here you can see that the first heaven is the earthly realm, or what you can see right now. Our bodies, our homes, and our cities exist in the earthly realm. Deuteronomy 10:14 says, "Indeed heaven and the highest heavens belong to the Lord your God, also the earth with all that is in it." According to the *New American Standard Exhaustive Concordance of the Bible*, the word *heaven* means, "astrologers, compass, Earth, heaven, heavens, and the highest heaven those, from the beginning, God created the earth, the heavens, and the highest heavens."[4]

The second heaven, or "mid-heaven" of Revelation 14:6, "and I saw another angel flying in midheaven, having an eternal gospel to preach to those who live on the earth and to every nation and tribe and tongue and people" (NASB), is the demonic and angelic realm where they war with each other. In Daniel, the second realm is also shown to be the demonic and angelic realm (see Dan. 10:13).

Then, there is the third realm. This realm is where the glory of God is. It's the beauty realm. The apostle Paul calls the third heaven "paradise." It's where we can see the great plans of Heaven.

> *I know a man in Christ who fourteen years ago—whether in the body I do not know, or whether out of the body, I do not know, God knows—such a one was caught up to the third heaven* (2 Corinthians 12:2).

He continues in verse 4, "...how he was caught up into Paradise and heard inexpressible words...."

The third realm is where every believer should live. You see, all believers should live from a place of victory, knowing and partnering with the strategies of God. Ephesians 2:6 says that God has "raised us up together, and made us sit together in the heavenly places in Christ Jesus." You have heard the saying, "so heavenly minded no earthy good"? That's a very impossible saying. I believe that, if you are heavenly minded, you will be of great good to this earth.

However, I've discovered that many intercessors do not live out of a place of joy because they get stuck in the first or second realms. When intercessors get stuck in the first realm, they are preoccupied with logic and reason. Then their prayers become focused on what *seems logical,* which is not where God is coming from most of the time! And then there are those intercessors who get stuck in the second realm. This realm is the dark and demonic realm, which produces hopelessness, doom, and fear.

The problem is that, when intercessors choose to pray from those realms, they end up praying from a defensive place. This is what it looks like. You are watching TV or reading the newspaper and some bad news comes across. You have just been made aware of the first realm (the physical realm). You become defensive in your prayers and pray on a human level. Or, you see into the demonic realm. Something bad is afoot. Sometimes it feels like pressure, like you have to pray now. It feels like you are chasing after the devil, and if you don't pray now, the whole world will be destroyed. I know that's a little extreme, but you get the idea.

I've learned that the devil will be more than happy to let us in on his schemes and strategies if it will distract us from what Heaven is doing. In the northern part of California, there is a beautiful mountain that is 14,000 feet from sea level, Mt. Shasta. Many people believe that the mountain carries power and consider it a high place of worship. There is a place on this mountain that is called Panther's Meadows. There is a spring there that bubbles up out of the ground and is the headwaters of one of our rivers. Unfortunately, this place is used for ungodly practices. Many years ago, as the story goes, a man went up to this meadow and had a visitation from a saint in the form of a black panther. Out of this vision came the name of this meadow and an international cult.

In finding out this information and realizing that this was a beautiful place that God had made, I thought it would be good to start taking teams up there to worship and pray. It had been used by so many to worship other gods that it should be a place of godly worship.

For one of those times, I felt that we were to go up the mountain and take communion, pray, and blow the shofar. I had around 150 people as a team that day, so it was a power-charged group, and they were ready to see God. We spent some time walking around the meadow praying, and then we gathered around the spring and took communion together. Then I had a friend blow her shofar. After the third blow on the shofar, we all shouted out praise to God. We thought we were the only ones on the mountain that day. We were wrong. As we all left the meadow and began to walk out, a few of us walked out the lower trail. As we walked out, we passed a tree, and we could hear someone hissing. All of a sudden, a young man jumped out from under the tree and ran as fast as he could past us and down the meadow. No sooner did this happen then we came upon a lady sitting *lotus style* (meditation form) trying to channel. When they channel, they use a coming noise, like a *shh, shh, shh*, repeating it slowly and softly. One of my friends who was with us had used this practice before she got saved, so she knew what was going on. This lady's air space had been so disrupted by our prayers that she was yelling her *shh, shh, shh*. My friend looked at me and said, "Well, she won't be getting anywhere today." Oh, to stop the plans of the devil—what a great day!

I love this story because it is a great example of how, as intercessors, we went to pray at a place that was known for its demonic activity, and we just focused on God. We were not distracted by the schemes of the enemy. All we did was look to God, and we let Him do the rest!

Jesus was the ultimate intercessor, and He saw right though the devil's tricks. The devil kept trying to bring Him into a dialogue about His identity. Jesus never went there. The devil was looking for just a little agreement. Don't you get the feeling that Jesus was in complete control of the conversation? He never once gave the devil fuel for his madness. In the first temptation, when the devil says, "If you are the son of God command this stone to become bread," he was trying to get Jesus to fight on his terms (see Matt. 4:3). Since Jesus was just finishing up a 40-day fast, it would have been really easy to do just that—turn the stone into bread to prove to the devil who He was. That would have been agreement with the devil. Jesus had no time for this realm of thinking. Jesus didn't even address the identity part of this question. Jesus knew who He was. He brought the situation right into a heavenly perspective: "It is written, man shall not live by bread alone but by every word of God" (see Matt. 4:4).

Jesus was completely human while being completely God. He chose this because He wanted to be the perfect example to us. He could have wowed the devil and us by turning that stone into a loaf of bread, but in order to be our perfect example, He showed us a better way to combat the enemy: "Let's bring Heaven in on this. What would Heaven say?" He was always looking in Heaven's direction.

Most assuredly, I say to you, the Son can do nothing of Himself. But what He sees the Father do; for whatever He does, the Son also does in like manner (John 5:19).

Being focused on the first and second realms brings us away from that third realm and keeps us focused on the devil or those things in life that trouble us. When we pray or prophesy out of the first two realms, we are not praying according to Heaven. Most of the time, we are praying out of fear. Prayers that are fear-based are not prayers that will produce a heavenly answer.

Can we know what is going on in those first two realms, or should we completely ignore them? It's OK to know what is going on, especially from the *second realm* (the demonic angelic realm). It makes us more informed in our prayers. Just get enough information to help. But we need to make sure that we do not live and pray out of those realms. Instead, we need to make sure that we remain focused on God and what He is doing. The key is to always ask God, "Father, what are you doing?"

I remember how excited I was when I began getting into historical research. (I call this prayer mapping.) I loved it! It almost became an obsession because I found myself spending so much time looking into the history of our region. As I began to study and study more, I noticed that I was getting more depressed. Then it hit me, "Oh, I'm getting too much information from the first and second realms and not enough from the third realm." Getting too much information can distract us from what we are supposed to be doing. So I began getting just enough information to be an informed intercessor.

When I am doing research now, I keep myself sensitive, and I can feel when I'm overdoing it. I can tell when I am not focused on the third heaven because the problem starts to look bigger than the answer. I cannot afford to be impressed with the devil. That overwhelming feeling starts to come, and I know it's time to stop. I've gotten enough information for the time being. Psalm 73 gives great understanding on the third realm, the heavenly realm. In the first half of the psalm, the writer is looking at those who prosper. He doesn't understand how they can be doing so well.

But as for me, my feet came close to stumbling. My steps had almost slipped, for I was envious of the arrogant as I saw the prosperity of the wicked (Psalm 73:2-3 NASB).

He was seeing through the first level of this world—*the physical realm*. He was looking into the wrong realm. What he was seeing was real, but he needed to understand it from another realm. Then, in verses 16 and 17, it starts to change:

> *When I pondered to understand this, it was troublesome in my sight until I came into the sanctuary of God; then I perceived their end* (Psalm 73:16-17 NASB).

Not until he goes into the sanctuary of God's presence does he understand what will happen to his enemies. Let me explain. In the Old Testament, the sanctuary was where the presence of God dwelt. "Let them construct a sanctuary for me, that I may dwell among them" (Exod. 25:8 NASB). When Jesus died for our sins and was resurrected, the Old Testament ended, and the New Testament began. When that happened, salvation happened. And now the presence of God dwells in us. Wow! How amazing that God would choose to live in our spirit man. We can now access that presence of God within us. We can say with the psalmist, from the deep place of our being, "You are continually with me."

> *When my heart was embittered*
> *And I was pierced within,*
> *Then I was senseless and ignorant;*
> *I was like a beast before You.*
>
> *Nevertheless I am continually with You;*
> *You have taken hold of my right hand.*
>
> *With Your counsel You will guide me,*
> *And afterward receive me to glory.*

Whom have I in heaven but You?
And besides You, I desire nothing on earth.

My flesh and my heart may fail,
But God is the strength of my heart and my portion forever.

For, behold, those who are far from You will perish;
You have destroyed all those who are unfaithful to You.

But as for me, the nearness of God is my good;
I have made the Lord God my refuge,
That I may tell of all Your works (Psalm 73:21-28 NASB).

You can see the psalmist's heart and mind change. You can see the understanding come after he has spent time in the third realm. Your perspective changes; it has to. Everything of weaker value that comes into the realm of God gets discarded. It becomes of no importance. All you want now is Him. You can say like the psalmist did:

Whom have I in heaven but You? And there is none upon earth that I desire besides You. My flesh and my heart fail; but God is the strength of my heart and my portion forever (Psalm 73:25-26).

It is not that the problems go away, but that you have a heavenly outlook now and understand that God has it all under control. This is also the place of authority for the believer—"seated in heavenly places in Christ" (see Eph. 2:6). It is not merely a place of divine perspective. It is the place of our enforcement of Christ's accomplishments at Calvary. My husband says it this way: "Look up before you look down." John 4:35 says, "Lift up your eyes and look at the fields, for they are already white for harvest." If we are looking up, we will see it the way God sees it. And God has an answer for everything.

ENDNOTES

1. George Otis Jr., *The Twilight Labyrinth* (Grand Rapids, MI: Chosen Books, 1997).

2. Francis A. Schaeffer, *Genesis in Space and Time: The Flow of Biblical History* (Ventura, CA: Regal Books, 1972), 62.

3. *New World Dictionary*, 2nd ed., s.v. "Realm."

4. *New American Standard Exhaustive Concordance of the Bible, Hebrew-Aramaic and Greek Dictionary*, Robert L. Thomas, Ed., version 2.2, s.v. "Heaven."

AIRWAYS

Those who own the airways control the atmosphere. The *airways* are the spiritual climate over a city. It is our responsibility to take ownership of the airways and reclaim the atmosphere. When we do that, a shift takes place in the spiritual climate in the region. When that shift takes place, we begin to see signs of revival, and entire cities become transformed by the things of God. When cities become transformed by the things of God, we see more light and less darkness in entire regions.

I'm a walker. I love to walk the land and pray and just enjoy the beauty of what God has given us. For a season, I would walk in just one area in our city. One day, during one of those walks, I felt like I was to ask the Holy Spirit what I should pray for that week. As I listened, I heard these words, "Pray for the communication lines."

What I felt was that I would pray that demonic communication lines would be severed.

So, not really knowing how to pray, but knowing that the Holy Spirit would enlighten me for that week, I finished my walk that morning with purpose to pray into this new strategy. When I got home that day, I turned on the television to watch *Fox News*. This was during the time when the Iraq war had just started. As I turned on the television, I heard these words, "The leader who is in charge of all the communications in Iraq has been arrested." Well, to say the least, I got very excited and knew once again that the Holy Spirit was confirming His words.

What I didn't know at the time was that this strategy for prayer would become one of the most important agendas in my prayer life—breaking demonic lines and releasing the pure godly lines of communication.

This was further illustrated to us on our trip to Mozambique in 2007. We were with Rolland and Heidi Baker of Iris Ministries. They had asked us to come to their staff retreat and had asked my husband Bill to speak to the group. Rolland, Heidi, and their staff from all over the world, meet once a year to soak and pray together and share life. It was an amazing time to sit and hear the miracles that were going on from all over the world. Our first night there, at dinner, we sat next to two women who had started a ministry with the children in Sudan. We listened for a good half hour as they poured out stories of great risk, courage, miracles, and healings with the children and themselves. It was astonishing to hear. Many would call them foolish to go into a country that is very volatile. I was so impressed with how excited they were.

They were born to see the Kingdom of God come on the earth, and you could tell.

In the course of our talking, one of the women mentioned *taking mountains*. She said in kind of a thought mode, "Those who take the airways own the atmosphere." I couldn't agree with that more. When I talk about airways, I'm saying that this is the spiritual climate over a city. There are spiritual powers that rule over cities and regions. These spiritual powers can control the atmosphere. Several years ago, I realized that we were taking control of the airways over our region. We were taking ownership of the atmosphere. Some of the things that we were seeing on our streets, with our ministry teams, included an increase in miracles, transformation in our schools, overall favor, and open doors into our city. There was a unity happening within our city government and the people of God. Many of our city government leaders are born-again believers. It's very easy to go into any eatery establishment and to see people with their Bibles on the tables or to hear conversations about what God is doing. Many of the stories that you will read in this book are the result of taking over the spiritual climate of our city.

War in the Heavenlies

Let's take a closer look in the Bible on this subject. In Daniel, chapter 10, Daniel received a message, but he needed understanding of the message. He went to fasting for 21 days. At the end of those 21 days, an angel came to him and said:

Do not fear, Daniel, for from the first day that you set your heart to understand, and to humble yourself before your

God, your words were heard; and I have come because of your words. But the prince of the kingdom of Persia withstood me twenty-one days; and behold, Michael, one of the chief princes, came to help me, for I had been left alone there with the kings of Persia (Daniel 10:12-13).

In Daniel's case, an angel was sent to give Daniel understanding about the message. But the ruling demonic prince held the angel back. He needed Michael, the warring angel, to come and fight this prince of Persia. The messenger angel was sent at the very beginning of Daniel's fast, but it took 21 days for the message to get through (with the help of Michael). There is a very real, invisible world around us, which does affect our visible world.

Now, let's take this even further so that we can understand how we can pray and allow this spirit realm to positively infect the physical world around us.

One of the beliefs that we have at Bethel is that we must infiltrate the system. We must be like good leaven. Matthew 13:33 says, "Another parable He spoke to them: 'The kingdom of heaven is like leaven, which a woman took and hid in three measures of meal till it was all leavened.'" As we put ourselves into our cities as leaven, it will affect the whole city and the atmosphere as well.

The Heartbeat of Heaven

Someone might ask, "How can we tell if we have taken the airways?"

When I was a little girl, I spent a lot of time just watching people. I was very curious. I believe that curiosity is a gift. It comes in very handy in the intercessory gifting. I still use this gift. You can find out a lot by just listening and watching, by paying attention to all that is going on around you and your city—reading articles in your newspaper, gathering little bits of information to let you know that God is moving and giving you ownership over your region. As an intercessor, you know the importance of finding the strategies of Heaven for anything that you are praying for, of making sure that the heartbeat of Heaven is in your praying. Don't you love that thought—"the heartbeat of Heaven"?

A gentleman in our church died for about four minutes and then came back to us. He said that he went to Heaven during that time. One of the things that he reported to us was that Heaven was loud, so loud that you had to have new ears. Heaven was full of intercession. That's when he started crying and told us not to stop interceding with Heaven. All of Heaven was interceding and interceding very loudly. If you have experienced that feeling, you know what Heaven is interceding. It's not just one thing; you can't pinpoint one thing. It's *all* things coming together in one heartbeat. One rhyme. It is ecstasy to hear that heartbeat.

When Change Comes

You will know when you pray with Heaven because when you do, you will begin to see changes. We have a ministry school at our church, Bethel School of Supernatural Ministry. I teach one of the advanced ministry training (AMT) classes on prayer and intercession. We meet together, I teach, and then we spend time going out and praying over different parts of our city.

I felt, during one of our prayer journeys, that we were to go to a vacant lot in the city and release a piece of land from a curse. For

years this land had been vacant. The story of this piece of real estate
is that it had once housed a bar where a lot of bad things happened.
Once, many years ago, a man who was drunk came out of the bar, got
in his car, hit a young girl, and killed her. This young girl's father
was a friend of one of the men in our church. The man in our church
was so grieved over this loss that, driving past the bar on his way
home one night, he looked over at the bar and said, "I wish that bar
would burn down." That night, the bar burned down. That happened
in the '70s, and from that time on, the lot stood vacant. I don't believe that praying the bar would burn down was the curse. I believe
the bar being there and the atmosphere that it brought caused the
land to be cursed. One day when I was praying about where to take
the students, I remembered this piece of land and the story behind
it. I felt like it was time that the curse be lifted off of this property.
The land needed freeing.

Going there would be a great opportunity for the students to
practice praying and releasing God's grace. The last day of my
AMT class, about 40 of us went to pray at this property. As we
drove up and parked, we noticed that there were two guys
across the street watching us. It's not every day that 40 people
drive up to a vacant lot, get out, and start walking and praying
out loud. I asked the students to just begin walking and praying
over the land. I released them to pray so that they would find
out what God was saying about the land. I took a couple of students with me, and we walked across the street to talk to those
two men. One was in a wheelchair. We asked if it would be OK
to pray for him. He said, "Yes." So we began to pray for his
healing. We also began to talk with them and let them know
what we were doing. We realized that this was a divine moment.
One of the men, when he found out what we were doing, said,

"Oh, I know about this place. My parents separated at this place when I was five years old." He also told us that three years ago he hit bottom and ended up at the homeless mission in town. He told us that shortly afterward, he got saved. God gave him a good job, and he attended our church. I had to leave and gather the other students for prayer, but I left the students that came with me to pray for those two men.

I gathered the students in a circle and had them declare what God was doing and, through the declaration, release the land from a curse. We believe in doing "prophetic acts" when we are praying. A prophetic act is doing something in the natural realm that brings a supernatural release. Doing an act like this causes an answer to come to the physical realm. So, we dedicated the land by pouring oil over it. We gave a shout of praise together that ended our time. I told them, "Now look for the answer."

Within a week, one of the students told me that, a few days after we prayed over our land, a gentleman went to the planning commission of our city and told them that he wanted to develop that land and put homes on the property.

That would be evidence of taking the atmosphere. That answer came so fast. By taking our students out that day, two things were accomplished: (1) they were given an accountable and safe environment to explore the ways of prayer, and (2) I believe that Heaven was moved to answer our prayers.

Can you just see what was taking place in the spirit realm? Use your imagination on this one and see what the angels were doing. They were released to do the plans of Heaven. It was like they were saying, "OK, now it's time. The curse has been broken.

We now have permission to work." I can see the angels coming to the man who wanted to develop this property and whisper in his ear, "You know that idea you have about developing the corner property? Now is the time to do that."

When you work and co-partner with God, the job gets done. This was one of those times when the answer came so quickly. A clearness in the spiritual communication lines brought quick results. How exciting to see! I have to tell you, though, that I knew that there would be a release, but I didn't know it would come so fast.

Effective Matter

We are a people who have the incredible opportunity to change our environment. We have living within us the Holy Spirit. Not only is the Holy Spirit power, but He is a lot of power. He is living in us so that we can be releasers of that power. He has put us here so that this world can have a power encounter with a heavenly God. I believe that there is so much power within us that, even when we die, we still carry that power. It is in our bones. Do you know that all matter has memory? One time I was researching the "memory of matter," and I found out that not just living matter but also dead matter has memory. Thinking about that, I traveled through the Bible in my mind trying to remember any stories that would confirm this finding. You remember the story of Elisha's bones? In Second Kings 13:21, they were burying a man, and suddenly they spied a band of raiders. They put the man in the tomb of Elisha, and when the man was let down and touched the bones of Elisha, he revived and stood on his feet. That healing power was still in the dead bones. That's just talking about dead matter. And in Luke 19:40,

Jesus tells the Pharisees that if His disciples didn't praise Him, the rocks would immediately cry out.

If all matter has memory, then that would mean that trees, plants, rocks, all have memory too. A good example of this occurred when I took some of our students out to pray—one of the students actually saw rocks manifest before her eyes. From time to time, we will take our students out on prayer trips to other smaller towns in our region. I had taken our students up to Mt. Shasta for a prayer walk through the town. We all divided up into small groups. I told them to walk the streets, go into the stores, and pray for God's blessing over the town. We believe that we are to bless people and their businesses. When we go out to pray over businesses, we release what God is doing. We do not curse a business, but we do believe that bringing blessing will stir up the spirit realm and bring God into the picture. I took one student with me, and we went into a new age store; there happened to be quite a few in this small town in Northern California.

As we walked into the store, I went one way and my young prayer partner went the other. After we got out of the store, she explained what happened to her. She had knelt down in front of a glass case that had beautiful, colored stones on the bottom shelf. She felt that she was to speak in tongues over the stones. When she stopped speaking in tongues, two of the stones began to vibrate. It obviously surprised her, so she tried it again to make sure she wasn't seeing things. It happened again. Now there's some matter with memory! Had those stones been dedicated for some ungodly purpose? I don't know. All I know is that when they came in contact with the realm of God, they had to cry out. When we carry the realm of God with us and do the things of the Kingdom, we will affect all matter around us.

Praying Over Fault Lines

We live in California, and as far back as my childhood, I remember hearing about California and earthquakes. I remember being on a Southern California beach when I was a teenager on the very day that the whole southern coastline was supposed to fall into the ocean because of an earthquake. These predictions concerning earthquakes in California, from both the secular world and Church, have been constant for many years. The Pacific Coast is part of the Ring of Fire. If you are not familiar with this, let me explain.

> The Ring of Fire is a zone of frequent earthquakes and volcanic eruptions that encircles the basin of the Pacific Ocean. It is shaped like a horseshoe and it is 40,000 km long. It is associated with a nearly continuous series of oceanic trenches, island arcs, and volcanic mountain ranges and/or plate movements. It is sometimes called the circum-Pacific belt or the circum-Pacific seismic belt.[1]

So you see why this is a constant issue with us who live here on the West Coast. We know that there is pressure under the earth and that it does need to be released. So our prayer has been, "God release it in small portions." God has and is answering our prayers and is giving us small portions of earth shakes.

In 2004, we were given another prophetic word that there was a big quake coming to California. For some reason, this word really shook me up. Now, remember that these have been frequent words for us here in California. When you hear these words over and over again, you have a tendency to just ignore them. This one was different. Maybe it was the person who was delivering the word. Whatever it was, it really disturbed me. I spent days just thinking and praying about the prophecy. One day while I was praying, a thought came to me to go to three areas down in Southern California. I called my friend, whom I had been discussing this whole prophecy with, and asked if she would go with me.

The three places we decided to go to in Southern California were Bakersfield, Lost Hills, and the top of the Grapevine (a stretch of Interstate 5 freeway). These three places were the ones highlighted to us. The San Andreas Fault line runs through these areas.

The San Andreas is the "master" fault of an intricate fault network that cuts through rocks of the California coastal region. The entire San Andreas Fault system is more than 800 miles long and extends to depths of at least 10 miles within the earth.

We decided to take a road trip and do some praying over the land south of us. The first spot that we chose was the top of the Grapevine. We spent the night at the top of the Vine. We felt like we were to blow the shofar that morning at sunrise. We have learned that blowing the shofar releases a sound into the atmosphere that breaks up the demonic and brings confusion to the enemy's camp. As we blew the shofar, my friend and I had a double vision (we both saw the same thing at the same time). We saw a large tube with dried old blood in it. As we blew the shofar, clean blood began running through the tube. We both knew that it was the blood of Jesus running through the region.

We did this in the next two locations as well. Our feeling of purpose for the trip was to quiet the fault line, to speak peace to it. Something had been spoken over our area that I didn't want to happen. God is waiting for us to take responsibility and to stand up and say, "Not on my watch!"

So I sought for a man among them who would make a wall, and stand in the gap before Me on behalf of the land, that I should not destroy it; but I found no one (Ezekiel 22:30).

He saw that there was no man, and wondered why there was no intercessor:

Therefore His own arm brought salvation for Him; and His own righteousness, it sustained Him (Isaiah 59:16).

Don't you love a good challenge? Both of these verses challenge me. To me, they are saying, "What are you waiting for?" Stand up and say to God, "Here; me; I'll do it; I will be the one who stands; I'll be the wall." I don't want God wondering why there is no intercessor. I want Him to be satisfied with what He sees in me. I get excited about that—about standing before God on behalf of injustice and unrighteousness.

There are times in prayer when I feel like I am standing as a wall between God and sin, crying out for God to have mercy. A way to explain this better comes from the days of old when people made fences using vines and hedges. When there was a hole or breach in the hedge, they would have someone stand there to protect the herds from harm until someone would come along to repair the breach.

*Therefore He said that He would destroy them, had not Moses His chosen one stood in the **breach** before Him, to turn away His wrath from destroying them* (Psalm 106:23).

Let's take a look at Moses for a moment. As Jesus is the great example of intercession in the New Testament, so is Moses in the Old Testament. There were many times that Moses would stand before God on behalf of a stiff-necked people. Let's look at a couple of those times.

The first story is the story of the golden calf. Exodus 32 tells us that Moses had been up on Mount Sinai and had been there for some time. The people became restless and decided to take things into their own hands. They had Aaron build them a god that would go before them. God could see all that was happening and got angry. He told Moses to get down off the mountain:

And the Lord said to Moses, "I have seen this people, and indeed it is a stiff-necked people! Now therefore, let Me alone, that My wrath may burn hot against them and I may consume them. And I will make of you a great nation."

Then Moses pleaded with the Lord his God, and said: "Lord, why does Your wrath burn hot against Your people whom You have brought out of the land of Egypt with great power and with a mighty hand? Why should the Egyptians speak, and say, 'He brought them out to harm them, to kill them in the mountains, and to consume them from the face of the earth'? Turn from Your fierce wrath, and relent from this harm to Your people. Remember Abraham, Isaac, and Israel, Your servants, to whom You swore by Your own self, and said to them, 'I will multiply your descendants as the stars of heaven; and all this land that I have spoken of I give to your descendants, and they shall inherit it forever.' "

So the Lord relented from the harm which He said He would do to His people (Exodus 32:9-14).

God had made a covenant with Abraham, Isaac, and Israel, a covenant that God swore by Himself, a covenant to multiply their descendants like the stars. Moses took that covenant and reminded God. Moses stepped into the breach that day. He filled the breach. He repaired the hole in the wall, so to speak. And, because of what Moses said, God changed His mind. Do you hear this? God changed His mind. That's amazing.

The Land of Promise

Another time that Moses made up the hedge was when God was giving the children of Israel the Promised Land. In Numbers 13 and 14, God sent in spies to see the land and how plentiful it was. Two of the twelve spies believed that the children could take this land, but the rest of the spies were afraid. The people sided with fear and refused to go into the land of promise. Intercessors must have faith. Faith looks at God. Fear only sees the impossible and the impossible becomes the reality. See what happens next:

Then the Lord said to Moses: "How long will these people reject Me? And how long will they not believe Me, with all the signs which I have performed among them? I will strike them with the pestilence and disinherit them, and I will make of you a nation greater and mightier than they." And Moses said to the Lord: "Then the Egyptians will hear it, for by Your might You brought these people up from among them, and they will tell it to the inhabitants of this land. They have heard that You, Lord, are among these people; that You, Lord, are seen face to face and Your cloud stands above them, and You go before them in a pillar of cloud by day and in a pillar of fire by night. Now if You kill these people as one man, then the nations which have heard of Your fame will speak, saying, 'Because the Lord was not able to bring this people to the land which He swore to give them, therefore He killed them in the wilderness.' And now, I pray, let the power of my Lord be great, just as You have spoken, saying, 'The Lord is longsuffering and abundant in mercy, forgiving iniquity and transgression; but He by no means clears the guilty, visiting the iniquity of the fathers on the children to the third and fourth generation.' Pardon the iniquity of this people, I pray, according to the greatness of Your mercy, just as You have forgiven this people, from Egypt even until now." Then the Lord said: "I have pardoned, according to your word (Numbers 14:11-20).

Look at that last verse (see Num. 14:20). God changed His mind because of what Moses said. Moses talked God out of killing the children of Israel. There was a huge breach, and Moses stood there until God changed His mind. I see an attitude in these two stories. We must take a stand and be like Moses. God had given him the promise, and even when God wanted to change His mind, Moses stayed firm. Moses carried faith and mercy with him, and because of that, he changed the atmosphere around him.

No Words Necessary

I have found that there are different ways to change the atmosphere. It doesn't always have to be with words.

> *Behold, as the eyes of servants look to the hand of their masters, as the eyes of a maid to the hand of her mistress, so our eyes look to the Lord our God, until He has mercy on us* (Psalm 123:2).

Look at the last part of this verse. They were just keeping their eyes on the Lord. No words were necessary. Just keeping focused on the Lord until....

We have many beautiful mountains around our city. One time we were heading to the top of one of them just to pray over our city. I had been wondering how we would pray when we got up there, asking God if there was anything I should bring to use as a prophetic act. I had made a shawl from purple material and a gold cord around the edges. I decided to take that shawl up to the top of the mountain.

The view from the top of this mountain was breathtaking. There was a lookout right at the top, and you could almost see all the way around the mountain from this spot. It was a gorgeous day. There was a breeze blowing. That day, all I knew to do was to stand at the edge of the mountain and lift up my purple shawl and let it blow in the wind. So there I stood with both hands up over my head, holding my purple shawl and letting it catch the wind. Doing this was a physical prophetic act. For me, the color of purple is royalty and intercession. The gold cord was the glory around the royalty and intercession. As it blew in the wind of

God, it was releasing over a region the royalty, intercession, and glory of the Kingdom. I know; it sounds a little crazy, but it sure felt good, and it was really fun. You might ask, "Did you really have to do that?" Well, maybe not, but I think that God likes what we do for Him, even if it looks a little crazy sometimes. Doing these acts may seem crazy or super spiritual to peers, but in doing these acts, I believe that we are standing as intercessors and that we are changing the airways around us.

ENDNOTE

1. "Pacific Ring of Fire," *Crystalinks*, http://www.crystalinks .com/rof.html (accessed 13 April 2008).

8

Warfare Through Worship and Joy

One day I was teaching in our supernatural school about intercession. At the end of my teaching, I asked if there were any questions. One of our young men, who we would have from time to time come up on the platform to dance during our worship, made the comment that he didn't think that he was an intercessor. I looked at him and said, "Are you kidding me?" I told him that he was an intercessor and that his intercession was the dance. You see, his idea of an intercessor was one who just used words to intercede. I explained to him that there are different types of intercession and that when he danced he was interceding. I told him that his intercession was the worship that became the warfare.

Two elements in warfare that I feel are our greatest tools of intercession are worship and joy. I believe that these two weapons bring more confusion to the devil's camp than anything else. Both of these weapons of war come out of our intimate relationship with our Father God. Let's explore these two weapons.

The Kiss

The Greek word for *worship* is *proskuneo;* it means "to kiss."[1] It is a feeling or attitude within us that keeps us close to God. It is not just about coming to church on Sunday and singing songs during the worship service. Even though that is an important thing that we do together, it is not the most important thing. Worship comes from within us and goes with us throughout our day. When we adore God, we are kissing Him.

Warfare worship is coming in on God's terms, not the devil's. We are focused on God, which ushers His power and presence into our intercessions. I was in one of our worship services one Sunday morning, and I kept getting distracted in my spirit. I felt like there were some witches in the room. I found myself completely out of worship. I remember, I kept turning around to look to see if I could figure out what was going on. I did this a few times. Then I heard Holy Spirit whisper, "You are being distracted from Me; just worship Me." It was a little nudge from the Spirit, but I got it. I realized that what I needed to do was just be with God and worship. He would take care of the spiritual matters in the room. My weapon of warfare that morning was to worship Him. God once spoke audibly to my husband saying, "He watches over the watch of those who watch the Lord." It is clear that having our eyes fixed on Him is our most responsible position, as God watches over the things that matter to us.

Just Worship

When we worship, we have access to the heavenly realm. When we worship, we push ourselves out of the inferior realms where we can pick up all of the negative stuff, and we end up in the glory realm, surrounded by His presence. I heard a story many years ago about a Christian man who was very depressed. He was so desperate for God to help him. He was crying out to God one day and heard the Lord tell him, "For a whole year, I want you to worship me." God went on to tell him that He didn't want him to ask for anything when he prayed. Just worship. After that year, he was released from the depression that he had lived in for so long. I'm sure he learned a very valuable lesson in that year.

Someone asked my husband what his prayer life looked like. He said, "If I have an hour to spend praying, I will usually worship for around 45 minutes and pray the rest." It's amazing how many things you can pray for in ten to fifteen minutes."

Worship Breaks Down Resistance

When we worship, we can release the presence of God and His Kingdom into the room. Years ago we were doing some meetings in Alaska. For several of the meetings, during the praise and worship time, there was no worship part. The praise was good, but we weren't getting to the intimate place of worship. It felt like there was a wall between us and God. We had brought our lead dancer with us on this trip. She is fun to take on trips because of the worship that she expresses when she dances. When we want something broken in the spirit realm, we have her get up and just worship. She doesn't dance to war, but her dance of worship becomes war. We don't even tell her what is going on. We just want her to worship. After being in a couple of these services in Alaska, my husband thought that it would be a good time for her to dance. She got up and began dancing, and whatever the wall was, it disappeared, and Heaven came into the room.

There was a gentleman at that service who could see into the spiritual realm. He was standing next to us while our dancer was up dancing. He told us after she finished what he saw. He had been watching demons in the room that night. They were sitting around the room. He said that when our dancer got up to dance, the demons began to scream, and they got out of the room as fast as they could. Yes, even in this we do not worship because of its effect on darkness; but we do so because God is worthy!

Worship, whatever form—dance, adoration that comes from our mouth, or any other kind of worship—terrifies the demonic realm. I believe they cannot stand to hear or even be close to those who are true worshippers. I've watched our son Brian take his guitar and play over a person in torment to see peace come. I know of a woman who goes to the convalescent hospital in our city and plays her flute over Alzheimer's patients to watch them become peaceful.

Let Worship Lead

Second Chronicles 20 gives us insight into a strategy where worship was used to win a battle. Jehoshaphat was faced with a great army coming against all of Judah. The first thing that Jehoshaphat did was to seek the Lord and proclaim a fast.

And Jehoshaphat feared, and set himself to seek the Lord, and proclaimed a fast throughout all Judah (2 Chronicles 3:20).

I like this verse because it says he "set himself" to seek the Lord. That means he set his face. I can see Jehoshaphet turning with an attitude of *I will not turn away until I have heard from God*. I like the courage and determination in this king's heart. The second thing that happened was that they prayed. The people came from everywhere to fast and ask the Lord what they should do.

So Judah gathered together to ask help from the Lord; and from all the cities of Judah they came to seek the Lord (2 Chronicles 20:4).

They began their prayer with adoring God for who He was and is.

O Lord God of our fathers, are You not God in heaven, and do You not rule over all the kingdoms of the nations, and in Your hand is there not power and might, so that no one is able to withstand You (2 Chronicles 20:6).

They were saying to God, "You are great and there is no one else."

Are You not our God, who drove out the inhabitants of this land before Your people Israel, and gave it to the descendants of Abraham Your friend forever?

And they dwell in it, and have built You a sanctuary in it for Your name, saying, If disaster comes upon us—sword, judgment, pestilence, or famine—we will stand before this temple and in Your presence (for Your name is in this

temple), and cry out to You in our affliction, and You will
hear and save (2 Chronicles 20:7-9).

It feels like they are reminding God of who He is and what He
has done for His people. It also looks like they are reminding
themselves of who God is and what He has done. That is a good
habit to have: always bringing the testimony of God before us to
remind us of His greatness.

In verse 9, Jehoshaphat talks about going into the temple and
into God's presence (see 2 Chron. 20:9). The prayer gets pretty
desperate in verse 12:

O our God, will You not judge them? For we have no
power against this great multitude that is coming against
us; nor do we know what to do, but our eyes are upon You
(2 Chronicles 20:12).

They basically said, "They are coming against us, and we just
don't know what to do, but our eyes are on You." Ever pray that
prayer? You just don't know what to do or how to even pray? At
times like this, such brokenness goes on in us. This brokenness
must lead us to God, not away from Him. We must set our eyes
upon the One who is true and trust Him. I think verse 13 is so key
for the Church right now. We are in a fight for the Kingdom of God
to be revealed.

Now all of Judah, with their little ones, their wives, and their
children, stood before the Lord. I believe that it is going to take
all of us, young and old, standing before the Lord in His presence, eyes set toward Him. We are all priests. Our little ones have

the power of God working in them to do great things for the King-dom, as there is no "Junior Holy Ghost."

Watch the Children

Every year during one of our conferences, we schedule prophetic booths. People can sign up for a time to meet with a team that we have picked to prophesy over them. In the last several years we have included our children to be on the teams. At first, people were a little skeptical until they sat down in the chair and a child would, as we say, "read their mail" and describe intimate details of their lives. Now when they come for prophetic ministry, they ask if the children are prophesying. We have found that the kids have a purity about their prophecies—nothing extra, just raw words from Heaven. When we look back into this story of Jehoshaphat, we see that Jehoshaphat knew that all the nation—men, women, and children—needed to be in on this prayer. It was a matter of life and death. They needed to stand together as one nation, one tribe, desperate for God to come. So God sent the prophet to tell the people what they needed to do:

> *Do not be afraid nor dismayed because of this great multitude, for the battle is not yours, but God's* (2 Chronicles 20:15).

The prophet then told them that they wouldn't have to fight in this battle but just position themselves, stand still, and see the salvation of the Lord. There are a lot of videos that I want to see when I get to Heaven, and this is at the top of my list because of what happens next.

The third thing that happened here in this story was that they worshipped the Lord.

God had answered His people, and in return, they bowed before the Lord and worshipped. There was a praise that rose up in the congregation. And, the fourth thing that happened was that they praised the Lord. That word *praise* is translated from the Hebrew word *tehillah* which comes from the Hebrew root word, *hallel*. *Tehillah* is "to praise" and *hallel* is "to be boastful, act insanely, drive madly, *giving praises*."[2] This was their time to let loose, to give wild praise to their God.

Jehoshaphat told the people to believe in the Lord and to believe in the prophets. He appointed those who should sing to the Lord and who should praise the beauty of holiness.

> *And when he had consulted with the people, he appointed those who should sing to the Lord, and who should praise the beauty of holiness, as they went out before the army and were saying: "Praise the Lord, for His mercy endures forever." Now when they began to sing and to praise, the Lord set ambushes against the people of Ammon, Moab, and Mount Seir, who had come against Judah; and they were defeated. For the people of Ammon and Moab stood up against the inhabitants of Mount Seir to utterly kill and destroy them. And when they had made an end of the inhabitants of Seir, they helped to destroy one another. So when Judah came to a place overlooking the wilderness, they looked toward the multitude; and there were their dead bodies, fallen on the earth. No one had escaped. When Jehoshaphat and his people came to take away their spoil, they found among them an abundance of valuables on the*

dead bodies, and precious jewelry, which they stripped off for themselves, more than they could carry away; and they were three days gathering the spoil because there was so much (2 Chronicles 20:21-25).

The result: God set ambushes so that, by the time the people of God got to the battle, the war was over. This is such an amazing story of a strategy of trusting God and letting praise and worship go before and win the fight.

They returned, every man of Judah and Jerusalem, with Jehoshaphat in front of them, to go back to Jerusalem with joy, for the Lord had made them rejoice over their enemies (2 Chronicles 20:27).

The people of God fought a war by worship. Their worship set in motion a shift in the heavenly realm, and God did the rest.

Warfare Through Joy

I believe we are to be a people that have Jesus' joy full in us. We are to be like that in every area of our life and ministry. One of the missing elements I see in many of those who are interceding is that they need their lives filled up with heavenly joy. I would love to go to Heaven for a visit and see just how joyful Heaven is. Their intercession in Heaven is not one of labor and work. There is none of that in Heaven. I think the intercession of Heaven is from a place of joy, a place of knowing.

For My yoke is easy and My burden is light (Matthew 11:30).

The *Message Bible* says it this way: "Keep company with me, and you'll learn to live freely and lightly."

Light and Easy

One of the men in our church came to me with a dream he had. He told me that he saw a river, and over the river, a group of women and I were walking suspended. We came floating over the river, laughing and filled with joy. We were taking care of problems with laughter and joy. It wasn't hard. There was a lightness to what we were doing. Along the riverbank there were broken crystal vases. We had a supernatural vacuum cleaner and just came along and vacuumed the brokenness away. He said that as he watched us, it seemed light, and we made it look so easy. I just laughed and said, "Yes, that's how we pray."

To some, that may seem like an impossibility. I would tell you that it is the most refreshing and effective way to war. One of the tricks of the enemy is to get us on his level, to get us to live on his playing field. Satan's world is full of labor and striving. If we step into that realm, we will only experience burnout. That's the plan of the enemy, to wear us completely out. It's not that we don't continually keep praying; it's our attitude in the continual prayer. Is there a striving in our prayers where we are doing all the work? Is there a weight that we carry around?

We learned a hard but very valuable lesson several years ago. There was a small group of women intercessors that I was really close to. One of the gals was a young Christian, new to intercession. In that season, the intercession was a lot of work and little relationship with the Father. When we went to church, we looked for problems and prayed against them. We spent all of our time looking away from Jesus. This was all we knew back then. We were just doing what we thought was our job. We felt like it was our responsibility to take care of all the demonic stuff that was going on in the room. I'll tell you, it was a lot of work, and we would go home tired and worn out.

One day I got a call from my friends, telling me that our young friend had left the church. She had had it and didn't want anything else to do with us. It was devastating to all of us. What had happened? What had caused this turn around in her life? Several months went by, and my husband was asked to speak at a church. The young girl had heard that we were coming and decided to come to church to hear Bill. At the end of the church service, the Holy Spirit started falling on people all over the building. This young girl ended up on the floor sobbing. I got down with her and just stayed there praying for her. I was able to ask her what had happened. Why had she left? The next words out of her mouth changed my life. She told me that she just got so tired of fighting and working in prayer that she just couldn't do it anymore. She thought that was the normal Christian life. It's all that she had ever seen. She just got burned out. She didn't realize that there was a place of joy to enter into and get refreshed; that's the place where we are to live.

I was so sorry for what had happened. A lot of repenting went on that day in my heart. To this day, that young girl has not returned to the church. Do I believe that she still loves God? Yes, I do. It's a sad story, but one I believe we need to hear. God wants to remove the stress and the striving from our intercessions. We need to keep filled up so that we won't burn out.

Defining Joy

But now I come to You; and these things I speak in the world so that they may have My joy made full in themselves (John 17:3 NASB).

To define joy, we would have to say that *joy* means "excitement or pleasurable feeling caused by the acquisition or expectation of good; gladness, pleasure, delight, exhilaration of the spirits."[3]

When we head out to pray over the land, we have done our research and know that there are things that have happened there that are bad. But, we also know that God is bringing something there that will change the spiritual climate of that area. That makes us very happy. Then we are able to go out with joy and release over the land what it needs. Joy comes when you have that feeling and expectation of good coming.

When you use joy in your warfare, it is because you are expecting good to happen. I took my interns to a Buddhist monastery in our area. I thought it would be a good experience for them to pray in a place where another god is served. We went there to pray. I had been to this place several times before and had found that it was an easy place to pray at. When we got there, I told them to just walk around and begin praying and feeling what God wanted to do. While we were having this time of walking, one of my interns came leaping by me, smiling and giggling. I like to call her Tigger. I love to pray with her because she is always finding God's heart. She told me in a singsong voice that there were a lot of demons here and that it was really easy to pray. When you experience God's presence around you, even in a demonic setting, you can find it easy to pray. Needless to say, we had a great time praying together that day. When you carry the joy of the Lord with you, all kinds of things happen. Joy brings excitement to the air, and it releases life. Really, it releases all of Heaven. I find myself, in the darkest places, getting so excited over what I sense God wants to release over a place or over a situation. We are releasers. We're meant to overcome the darkness with light. Do you want to bring confusion to the darkness that is trying to rule over you and others?

In Him was life, and the life was the Light of men. The Light shines in the darkness, and the darkness did not comprehend it (John 1:4-5 NASB).

That means that the darkness cannot overtake the light. It doesn't understand it. Darkness looks at light and gets all confused. Just knowing that when you pray will give you a joy that will burst from you. The New King James Version *Spirit-Filled Life Bible* says, regarding the word *comprehend*, "The Christian's joy is in knowing that light is not only greater than darkness but will also outlast the darkness.[4]

Joy, the Element of Surprise

Let's talk about "warfare through joy" and using it as "the element of surprise."

In wartime, you have to use one very important principle: the element of surprise. In the magazine, *The Armchair General*, Robert R. Leonhard writes:

Surprise is a viable principle of war. Techniques for delaying the enemy's detection include using stealth, camouflage, deception, operational security measure, and the indirect approach. An ambush, for example, aims to overwhelm the enemy not just with weapons fire, but also with confusion, noise, and fear.

Surprise, then, is a principle of war that is alive and well. It is an enduring feature of warfare, because its components-time and perpetual unreadiness are immutable. Just as they have done throughout history, commanders will continue to seek ways to delay detection, hasten contact, and vary the method of attack in order to expose the enemy's unreadiness, turn the enemy's time flank, and win.[5]

That's how I feel about "warfare through joy." It is like the element of surprise. I believe that this joy brings confusion to the enemy's camp. The enemy doesn't know how to combat joy in a person. This joy catches the demonic realm completely off guard. We have a prayer meeting at our church on Sunday night before the service. It's called our pre-service prayer. I love to watch the visitors come to this meeting. It really should be called the happy prayer meeting.

Good Medicine

When you come into the room, you will be met by people who are sitting, lying on the floor, or walking in a circle around the room. Some people will be walking with their arms around their friends, some will be lying on the floor soaking in His presence, others will be sitting and reading their Bibles. The reason I like to watch the visitors is because I don't think that many of them have ever been in a prayer meeting quite like this one before. Sometimes it appears that they don't know what to do or how to act. It's definitely not a time for being serious. It's a time for joy in the house. Usually, by the time we finish, there are people all over the floor, and better yet, laughing people all over the room. We feel that the angels really like that atmosphere and seem to show up and have fun, too. The way we fight is a lot of joy! Laughter is good medicine.

A merry heart does good, like medicine, but a broken spirit dries the bones (Proverbs 17:22).

The definition for the word *merry* is "in overflowing good spirits; hilarious; mirthful; gay and noisy."[6]

I know of a pastor that will have a group of his people sit in a circle. They will go around the circle and share their problems. When they are done, he will have them laugh at the problems. They will laugh until they get it and their problems don't seem so big and overwhelming.

Researchers from the University of Maryland School of Medicine in Baltimore compared the effects of watching funny and stressful films with these results:

Stress caused blood flow to slow by around 35%, but laughter increased it by around 22%, they told the American College of Cardiology.

Michael Miller, director of preventive cardiology at the University of Maryland Medical Center, who led the research, said: "The endothelium is the first line in the development of atherosclerosis or hardening of the arteries, so, given the results of our study, it is conceivable that laughing may be important to maintain a healthy endothelium, and reduce the risk of cardiovascular disease.

"At the very least, laughter offsets the impact of mental stress, which is harmful to the endothelium." He added: "Thirty minutes of exercise three times a week, and 15 of laughter on a daily basis is probably good for the vascular system."[7]

*You have turned for me my mourning into dancing; You have loosed my sackcloth and girded me with **gladness*** (Psalm 30:11).

ENDNOTES

1. "The New Testament Greek Lexicon," *Studylight.org*, s.v. "Proskuneo," http://www.studylight.org/lex/grk/view.cgi?number=4352 (accesssed 18 Sept 2008).

2. *New American Standard Exhaustive Concordance of the Bible, Hebrew-Aramaic and Greek Dictionary*, Robert L. Thomas, Ed., version 2.2, s.v.v. "Tehillah," "Hallel."

3. *The New Webster Encyclopedic Dictionary of the English Language*, s.v. "Joy."

4. *Spirit-Filled Life Bible* (Nashville: Thomas Nelson Publishers, 1991).

5. Robert R. Leonhard, "Surprise," *The Armchair General*, LTC, www.jhuapl.edu/areas/warfare/papers/surprise. pdf (accessed 13 April 2008).

6. *The New Webster Encyclopedic Dictionary of the English Language,* s.v. "Merry."

7. "Laughter 'boosts blood vessels,'" *BBC News*, March 7, 2005, http://news.bbc.co.uk/2/hi/health/4325819.stm (accessed 13 April 2008).

The Rest That is Internal

One hand full of rest is better than two fists full of labor and striving after wind (Ecclesiastes 4:6 NASB).

True heavenly experiences are always life changing. When I am having such an experience, it feels as though my whole being is awakened to that moment. Recently, I experienced a heavenly encounter where Jesus picked me up and swirled me around. Immediately, we were standing in front of a cottage that looked like a little English cottage with an English garden in the front. He carried me under a beautiful flowered arbor. He then put me down onto a walkway leading to the cottage. I knew that this was my cottage. I was standing there looking and from around the side yard came all of the grandchildren. Our oldest grandchild, Kennedy, came up first, and I heard her say, "Oh good, Grandma's here; now we can play." Then they all ran off to play. The next feeling I had was that I was in the midst of all my relatives. I could not see them all, but I knew they were there. Another feeling I had was that this was the end of time; we were all in Heaven and earthly time had ended.

Then, from around the left side of me, appeared one of my grandmothers, whom we called "Granny." Granny was a large woman with big features, and boy, could she laugh. She was married to a preacher, and their life was hard. There was a lot of bitterness in her life that I believe physically harmed her body. Before she died, she let all that hurt go. But, above all of the hurts in her life, Granny knew how to laugh and have a good time. She would throw her head back and open her mouth so wide that you could see her tonsils, and then she would let out a big laugh. All enjoyed the moment. When I saw her in this heavenly place, as I looked over at her, she tipped her head back and let out one of those laughs. It was just the way that she had always laughed. She was Granny. I thought, "Oh, she is having a good time in Heaven."

No sooner had I seen my granny than I looked behind me and saw my other grandma, my dad's mom. One of the things my grandma loved to do was teach Sunday school. She taught for 25 years. The Sunday morning that she retired from teaching Sunday school, the church had an honoring time for her. While she was up on the platform, she collapsed from a stroke. Five days after her stroke, she was in Heaven. As I turned to look at my grandma, there she was with all of these children around her. I got so excited for her because she was doing the very thing she enjoyed so much here on earth.

While this was all going on, there was a feeling that I had experienced before when I had been in God's presence. It was peace. But this time it was different. It was the most complete peace that I had ever felt. Let me explain. What made this peace feel different was that my head was clear. There was no stress, no pressure from all of the things that clutter our minds. It was all gone. It so undid me that I was crying like a baby through the whole vision—not a sad cry, a joyous cry. I thought, "This is Heaven. This is what it feels like when you are in Heaven." Can you imagine what it will be like when we are in Heaven forever and all the clutter that fills our lives is gone? That's peace. It's the rest of Heaven. It is so complete that there is nothing you want more than that.

A Place of Rest

Isn't it funny that the word *restless* comes from the word *rest*. *Restless* means less rest. I remember one time when I felt as though I was carrying so much responsibility in prayer. At that time, I had one of our students come up to me one day and tell me basically that it was all right, that I didn't have to feel or carry all the responsibility of prayer. That word was so encouraging to me that day because that was what I was walking in at that moment. It hit me like a breath of fresh air. I received the word and came back into a place of rest. It doesn't mean that I stopped praying for what was on my heart. But, it took me out of the striving and performance that can wrap itself around our prayer agendas (faith is more the product of surrender than it is of striving).

There is a mindset of performance that can grab hold of us and push us to do things for God that He is not asking us to do.

When that happens, it takes us right out of rest. We can feel like we need to do for God so that He will approve of us. We think by doing this God will accept us more and maybe love us more. I'm telling you, you don't have to do a thing for God, and He will love you no less. So many of us have believed that we need to labor and perform for God so that we can gain an identity, so that we might be accepted. But in the Kingdom we start off accepted. From there our identity is formed. As intercessors, we need to pray out of that new identity, that core belief that says, "I am already accepted! I am already loved! I already have favor with God!" You see, we are already accepted. Unfortunately, many of our life experiences do not teach us this. In life, you get rewarded or receive approval if you do this or that. The Kingdom of God doesn't work that way. God is not sitting up in Heaven waiting to love you if you will do something for Him. He is a lot more interested in our entering into His love and rest. Let's take a deeper look into the rest of the Lord.

The True Sabbath

When you were dead in your transgressions and the uncircumcision of your flesh, He made you alive together with Him, having forgiven us all our transgressions, having canceled out the certificate of debt consisting of decrees against us, which was hostile to us; and He has taken it out of the way, having nailed it to the cross. When He had disarmed the rulers and authorities, He made a public display of them, having triumphed over them through Him. Therefore, no one is to act as your judge in regard to food or drink or in respect to a festival or a new moon or a Sabbath day—things which are a mere shadow of what is to come; but the substance belongs to Christ (Colossians 2:13-17).

This tells us what Jesus did when He came and gave up His life for us. He canceled the bond—all those rules and regulations that were a legal binding. It was all nailed to the cross. Principalities and powers were disarmed. Our Christ triumphed over all. So the true Sabbath becomes the rest of God. As God rested, and then as Jesus finished His work and rested, we too can enter into a true rest.

There remains therefore a rest for the people of God. For he who has entered His rest has himself also ceased from his works as God did from His (Hebrews 4:9-10).

The meaning of the word *rest* in both the Hebrew *(shabath)* and Greek *(katapausis)* is to "cease, celebrate, desist from exertion, leave, put away, reposing down and abode."[1] I believe that the true Shabbat rest means to cease from your labors, your own efforts, your own activities. I am not implying that you stop your ministry or working for the Kingdom. What I am telling you is that you must have the heart of rest. That means ceasing from your own efforts, your own striving, and depending on the works of another: God. Whenever I begin to get that overwhelming feeling and I feel the striving coming on, I stop myself and enter right back into the rest of the Lord. When we walk in this rest, we live our lives more fully, and we are more effective in our ministries and giftings.

Keeping Your Rest

As intercessors, if we want to stay in a place of rest, we have to learn how to pray and do our part and to then give our burdens back to the Lord. Our daughter, Leah, was a nanny for five years. She started overseeing two girls who were amazing. One of the little girls could see into the spirit realm. She was able to use her sense of feeling and her sense of seeing to understand what was going on. I called Leah one day and asked if they could go out to eat. We met at one of the local restaurants for lunch. As we walked into the restaurant we noticed that (we will call her) Rachel started hiding behind Leah. When we got to the table, she was pretty disturbed and kept turning around. I asked her what was the matter. She told me that the lady sitting behind us was sad, that her heart hurt. Rachel was only three at the time. I realized that Rachel was seeing into this person's life. So, we prayed right there and asked Jesus to help this lady and heal her heart. Rachel was still upset. So I told her that we would pray one more time. We did, and then I told her that we had to give this feeling to Jesus and let it go. We did, and Rachel was fine and returned to her happy self. I sat there amazed and thought to myself, "I wish that I could have learned that lesson when I was young. That lesson would have saved me a lot of internal heartache."

I believe it is possible to carry rest with us because God is not asking us to carry the world on our shoulders. He is asking us to enter into a rest that is internal. My husband is, I think, one of the busiest people on the planet. It is a challenge for him to get the rest he needs. But, the one thing that I have noticed through our years together is that he carries an internal rest of the Lord. It is very strong in him. He knows where his source is, and he draws from it often. If he didn't have that inner strength, there is no way that he could carry on with his life. We have no plan "B." God is our plan "A," and He is our source.

"Come to Me, all who are weary and heavy-laden, and I will give you rest. Take My yoke upon you and learn from Me, for I am gentle and humble in heart, and you will find rest for your souls. For My yoke is easy and My burden is light" (Matthew 11:28-30 NASB).

Rest is mentioned twice in these verses. The first time Jesus is saying, "Come all who are weary and heavy and I will give you rest" (see Matt. 11:28). The second time He tells us, "You will find rest" (see Matt. 11:29). We come to Him first, and He gives us that rest. Then, as we continue to take on His yoke, we will learn from Him. It's the school of the Holy Spirit that we have entered into. As we grow in Him and His ways, or even His presence, we will then find rest for our souls.

Jesus gave us an example of this in Matthew 8.

Resting in the Storm

Now when He got into a boat, His disciples followed Him. And suddenly a great tempest arose on the sea, so that the boat was covered with the waves. But He was asleep. Then His disciples came to Him and awoke Him, saying, "Lord, save us! We are perishing!" But He said to them, "Why are you fearful, O you of little faith?" Then He arose and rebuked the winds and the sea, and there was a great calm. So the men marveled, saying, "Who can this be, that even the winds and the sea obey Him" (Matthew 8:23-27).

As we read this story, we have to wonder how Jesus slept in a storm when it looked like all were going to perish. Jesus even asked them after they cried out to Him, "Why were you fearful, O

143

you of little faith" (see Matt. 8:26). Jesus lived in an internal security. It was so strong in Him that nothing could shake Him from that reality. Jesus could sleep in a storm. He practiced and modeled for us in this story, giving us an example of what it looks like to have rest of the heart.

A Simple Thing

But even though we can carry the rest of God with us, we still have to learn how to enter His rest. I remember one of the first times that I began to practice moving into the rest of God. It was a few years ago, and I had driven into town to do some shopping. On that hour-long drive, the vehicle that I was driving decided to give up and quit. My first response was to panic and get really mad. "How could this happen? Everything is now messed up for the day." You know how we carry on sometimes. I found a pay phone (no cell phones then) to call my husband. As I began to dial the number, I thought to myself, "Why am I acting this way? Why am I so upset?" Then I realized something that was so simple but that changed my life. Sometimes it's the simple things in life that make that change for us in our thinking. I thought, "You know, I think that if I settle down and come to rest inside, I will be able to see what God can do in this situation." So, I made a simple choice and decided to let God have this little mess of a day. Of course, once I made that decision, everything lined up and worked together. I chose the "rest of the Lord" that day for my life. I think about that day often. In what seemed like a trivial thing, God let me see that I could draw from His rest anytime I needed. It was my choice.

You ever play the "what if" game? For example, what if the disciples would have made a choice and stepped right into that rest that Jesus had? What would have happened in this story? What if you step right into the "rest of the Lord" right now? What would happen? The story of your life would be quite different, wouldn't it be?

God is calling us to choose His rest and to cultivate it in all that we do.

ENDNOTE

1. *New American Standard Exhaustive Concordance of the Bible, Hebrew-Aramaic and Greek Dictionary,* Robert L. Thomas, Ed., version 2.2, s.v. "Rest."

ADDRESSING THE ISSUES

I spent two years of my life crying just about every time I went to church, feeling and knowing things in the spirit world. Sometimes I would cry because I could feel the presence of the Lord so strongly in the service. I spent much of that time caught up in glorious and heavenly encounters. But how many know that, if you cry in a public place for any length of time, people begin to wonder about you and to wonder what is happening? I remember that many people came to ask me if I was doing all right during that season. I told them that I was really feeling God, and I told them what He was doing. But I think it was really hard for people to understand that the season of crying that I was experiencing was not a bad thing. From the outside, it probably looked like there was something wrong. But for me, it felt like things could not be any more right.

During that season, there were times that I would just go hide behind the stage and intercede. It was an amazing time of learning for me and for others. God started moving in amazing ways in our services. It was during this time that the intercession at our church really became strengthened. But I want to make it clear that we did not pray in revival. We did not have special prayer meetings where we prayed that revival would come. For us, revival came, and then we started having prayer meetings. God just came and moved and from that, all of our intercession grew.

The ministry of intercessory prayer within the church is a helping ministry. We as intercessors are to pray for the pastors and leaders as well as the ministries of the church. We are there to bless the leadership, to pray over their ministries that they would expand and be blessed and grow, and to pray for protection over them and their families. As intercessors, we are there to make things easier for the leaders. That's what we felt like we were doing. We felt like we were helping.

During this time, we felt like we were to have intercessors praying during the services. We set up intercessors to cover the worship team and to cover the speaker during the services. We were praying for blessing, for the anointing, and for God to come. So we started assigning people to pray behind the stage on Sundays. God was just pouring out, and we were agreeing with Him, and we didn't want to miss out on anything that He was doing. Those intercessors became a covering for the worship team as well as the speaker for that Sunday.

Confronting the Bad Dreams

I remember that a lot of people started picking up "negative things" during that time. I think of negative things as dreams, visions, and thoughts that do not reveal the plans that God has to bless the earth. You see, people were picking up dreams, vision and thoughts from the second realm. People were coming to me with so much negativity that I felt like we were not seeing correctly. When I went to the Holy Spirit for counsel and understanding, I felt like He told me that He was allowing this information to come out because He wanted us to learn how to pray from Heaven's perspective. So when people would come to me with the negative, second realm feelings and insights, I would tell them that God was allowing them to see this for a reason. It was now their responsibility to see this from Heaven's perspective. I told them that they needed to ask God what He was up to. You see, when you see something negative, you always need to go to God and say, "OK, God, what are you doing? What are you saying through this? How do you want me to pray?"

It is always easy to find dirt. But God wants us to look past the dirt and to look for the treasure. The Scriptures say,

It is the glory of God to conceal a matter, but the glory of kings is to search out a matter (Proverbs 25:2).

Seeing God's Way

Let me give you an example of searching out the treasure. One Sunday morning, I found myself on the floor with God. He brought a picture of a man who owned one of the tattoo parlors in town. I had seen this young man at his shop one day. I could read him by just looking at him. The eyes tell you all you need to know.

That's what I saw that Sunday morning. I saw the hate and anger. Instead of cursing the man and cursing his business, I began to see God's heart for him. Oh my, I was so undone. I prayed his destiny over him and prayed for God to pour His love out on him and to take the hate and anger. I have never heard if that young man changed his ways or if the hate and anger left. But, because of the intense time of prayer, I know that God was up to something that morning. I was the one standing in the gap for that man, pleading his case before God. Allow God to grab your heart. Let Him take you to a place of intercession. Be still and know that He is God. When I was praying for that young man, I was seeing him the way God saw him. It's what we call "finding the gold in someone."

In finding the gold in someone, you have to dig deeper. It's never hard to find dirt, but we must go deeper to find the gold; that's seeing a person the way God sees him or her. When we see bad stuff around us, all we need to do is go deeper in God and find the gold. Find the things that God is saying. Then we can come into agreement with the gold. Wow! What a concept, praying Heaven!

As an intercessor, I want the leaders I am praying for to feel like I am a blessing and not a burden. I met with a pastor one afternoon to talk. After I spoke at his church, I asked him how his relationship with his intercessors was. He said to me, "Do you really want to know?" I told him, "Yes." He said, "To be honest with you, they exhaust me." He continued, "They are bringing me all their dreams, their warnings, what should happen here, and it's so much, I just get worn out." I suggested to him that he have one head intercessor and that perhaps once a month he should go in and talk with the intercessory group and keep connected with them. Having one head person is so helpful because he or she can lead the group with the pastor's covering. Then if the head intercessor feels a need to come to him for anything, he or she can.

Don't Be Offended

We live in such a prophetic culture that, if we turned our people loose on any given Sunday, we would be there all day just to hear what God was saying. I remember when we first came to Bethel, on Sunday mornings, we would have many people come up with a prophetic word or a feeling of what we should do next in the service. It was our job to try and figure out which ones to use and which ones to leave. During that season, we discovered that it is the responsibility of the leader to decide what to do with the prophetic word or direction that an intercessor brings to us, and not the intercessory person.

I know that time was hard for some because we would not always use what they would bring us. But, this is a good lesson for us as intercessory people under a leader to learn. As intercessors, we come with what we feel is a word or direction from God and give it to our leaders. Then, we must trust them to do what they think is best. There must be a relationship that is filled with trust between the pastor and intercessor. Remember intercessor, you are coming along to help the pastor or leader. You are coming alongside to pray protection over them.

The Art of Intercession

We believe that releasing intercession through the arts is a very important part of our prayer at Bethel. We have two forms of prayer that are used to model how the arts and intercession flow together.

Below is a description of our platform intercession:

> The intercessors we draw from for a service are individuals who are moved specifically by intercession through worship, people who want to partner with God to see the very atmosphere changed when they step into a place of worship. Our teams are encouraged to respond creatively through worship to release the movements of Heaven, as if to release a physical demonstration of what is felt in the atmosphere.

> Teams are developed by relationship and staying connected with each other. It is my belief that as we walk in relationship and understanding, when a change in the atmosphere occurs, we will sense it easier and be able to respond accordingly in unity. The intercessors are designed to be in relationship with the worship teams and to cover them in prayer. In building relationships we will be able to move in unity and as one in the Spirit with a greater authority.

> As a leader I am blessed to have intercessors that come filled up and ready to give, who are excited and expecting that God is good all the time and are anticipating new things. We at Bethel promote joy and want to be releasers of God's love. We show up one hour before the service and start to pray for the worship musicians while they are practicing. This allows the team time to connect in the Spirit with the musicians and with what God is

about to do for the service. During worship practice the leader will pray and get a sense of where to position team members. I feel it's important when it comes to placement of intercessors, that the leader release authority and a covering to each member. Since we have more than one service, we have several leaders within the entire group. The lead intercessor is always placed behind the worship leader. Intercessors are placed next to the worship team with an understanding that everyone has his or her own spiritual space, again reinforcing the need for relationship with each other.

After worship is over we meet as a group and pray together and cover each other for the week to come. Having your intercessors covered by authority is the most important gift that you can give them.

I use the same principle for art as intercession. With our artists I encourage individuals to move through their art as if their painting is a reflection of what is going on in the Spirit.

Always looking to capture the unseen realm when we paint from Heaven's perspective, we begin to move in God's healing and deliverance. We are learning to release movement of sounds, colors, and painting pictures that encourage angelic visitations. It is my desire to reveal God's heart and truth through art, to inspire others to live their lives free from limitations that keep them in the natural dimensions of this world. What if we could move from bondage to freedom because of a painting? What if a picture of an angel would release a visitation from God? I have now witnessed artwork that has been painted from a heavenly encounter that speaks to me, confirming in my spirit. God is continually showing up in all the arts, and He has a lot more to express through the arts.

At times artists will have dreams and visions that take them into a place I like to call living art, art that is inter-active and comes to life. Here the artists enter into the very art work itself and it is as if they become a part of the painting. Other artists will get downloads of colors. They begin to release them into the atmosphere and grab hold of what is happening in the supernatural. To those who are unfamiliar with art as intercession, they think of it as just colors and movement, but with every sound, a color is released and a chance to experience a new realm of God's creativity.[1]

During one of our conferences, we were alerted by some of our friends who had friends in Fiji that a tsunami was coming into the Fiji Islands. We felt like it was very important to pray for this. So we corporately began praying. During this prayer time, someone noticed a painting on the platform that one of our intercessors had painted the night before. He ran up on the platform and brought the painting out to the front for all to see clearly. The painting was a picture of a huge wave cresting and coming onto a land mass. But, between the huge wave and the land, was a very large brick wall. It looked as though the wall was put there to stop the wave. To say the least, we were all amazed. This painting had be-come our prayer. Our prayer surged that morning. Our faith level hit the roof because we knew that God would stop that tsunami.

There was no doubt in our minds. Just shortly after we prayed, we received word that what was to be a destructive wave dissolved to nothing. We felt through the painting that God had already seen the problem coming and had already given us the answer.

Another area of prayer and creative arts that we have seen take off is a ministry called 48HOP, a 48-hour prayer time that involves art expression.[2] Our oldest son, Eric, felt the need to start a prayer meeting that would go 48 hours in his church. From there it evolved into a ministry and has gone to several places around the world. His heart was to see all people, not just those who call themselves "intercessors," drawn into a lifestyle of prayer.

Some friends of his showed him a passage, Zechariah 1:18-21:

Then I raised my eyes and looked, and there were four horns. And I said to the angel who talked with me, "What are these?" So he answered me, "These are the horns that have scattered Judah, Israel, and Jerusalem." Then the Lord showed me four craftsmen. And I said, "What are these coming to do?" So he said, "These are the horns that scattered Judah, so that no one could lift up his head; but the craftsmen are coming to terrify them, to cast out the horns of the nations that lifted up their horn against the land of Judah to scatter it" (Zechariah 1:18-21).

So 48HOP involves doing a lot of things with art, music, and creativity. As you come into the room, it is filled with live music and/or CDs playing worship. All around the room there are prayer stations. There can be a station where you sit and paint as an act of worship or intercession. There can be a canvas with the world drawn out on it. People can come to this canvas and with a

Sharpie pen write prayers over different parts of the world. Another station will have a folder with prophetic words in it for people to read and pray over. There is a journaling station where you can make a prayer journal of your prayers while in the prayer room. There is a creative writing station where you can sit at a table and express yourself with writing to God. Then, from time to time, we have a leader come up and lead in corporate prayer. There is an open mic, and people can come up and pray according to what is being prayed for at that time.

What is so wonderful about this event is that people who would normally not give themselves to prayer and intercession find prayer in their art expressions. We have had people tell us that this has caused their prayer life to come alive. Prayer never has to be boring. The children love 48HOP. I remember one time when we had it at the church that one of our elementary teachers brought in her first grade class. The worship music was playing and she had them all lie on the floor and soak in God's presence. It was an amazing sight. Then, after a few minutes, she released the children to go to one of the stations to pray with creative expression.

In the *Shepherd's Rod 2005*, Bob Jones and Paul Keith Davis mention that the "Host of Heaven" is going to come to houses of prayer. At the end of one of the 48HOPs, our son was starting to close it up but didn't really want to end the time because the host of Heaven had not visited this house of prayer. So he, along with three others, stayed past the 48 hours slotted for that event. He was on the piano worshiping, and something began to take place in the room. Angels began to show up all over the room. There were streaks of gold and white across the room. Flashes of light began to appear in different areas of the room. He could tell when the angels entered the room because they were coming through the back door, and when they did enter, the doorway would bow and flex. These angels began to walk up and down the aisles of the seats. Their feet were visible and they were very busy and walking fast all around the room. His estimation was that there were 30 to 40 angels in the room. They were there for business; they were there to establish the glory of God. This went on for around 30 to 45 minutes. It was a good night.

God has released His people to live with expression and to be releasers of that expression. It is no different with prayer. We should be able to show different types of prayer expressions, whether it is in an art form, word form, or some other form.

Prophetic Intercession

Below is a description of our intercessory group at the church.

We have a large group of organized intercessors within the church. Our intercessors are taught to wait for the Holy Spirit and to ask for His leading. The Bible says,

> *Likewise the Spirit also helps in our weaknesses. For we do not know what we should pray for as we ought, but the Spirit Himself makes intercession for us with groanings which cannot be uttered* (Romans 8:26).

One of the things that is so fun about our intercessors' meetings is that, because our intercessors wait on the direction of the Holy Spirit before they begin to pray, every meeting is different. The Holy Spirit is so progressive and creative! Our intercessors spend time soaking in the presence of the Holy Spirit before they begin to pray. They wait on Him as they prepare their bodies, souls, and spirits to work together as one. Our intercessors find out what He is doing before they begin to pray.[3]

Honor

I believe that one of the things that makes our groups of intercessors so successful is that they have trust and honor from the leadership within the church. Through relationship, we know as leaders that we can turn this ministry over to a group of very devoted people, and we know that they will carry our vision.

A Good Report

I had a young man come up to me at the end of one of our conferences. He was visiting and had the opportunity of spending time with some of our intercessors. He told me that he had enjoyed being with our intercessors because they were so happy. They were so full of joy. I told him that this was our DNA. It was the best compliment that I could have received.

We are to be a people full of Heaven, and Heaven is a place that is full of joy.

Pastors, I encourage you to honor and develop trust with those in your church who are intercessors. They may be a little wild and seem to do some crazy, symbolic, prophetic stuff, but if you will give them covering and let them fly, they will be dedicated to you to the death. Intercessors, if you will come under your leadership and submit your ministry of prayer and service, you will find fulfillment that you have been longing for. It is worth working for relationship between pastor and intercessors.

Witchcraft Prayers

Have you ever heard this prayer coming out of someone's mouth that sounds something like, "God, I ask that you would teach my pastor and show him that he needs to change his way of thinking." That is a prayer of manipulation and control. That is the nature of witchcraft. Witches control by casting spells on people or things. Trying to control comes out of a fear of being controlled yourself. It comes out of insecurity. Praying controlling prayers is dangerous. Many don't even realize what we are doing when we try and control with our prayers. There is a line that we can cross when we decide that we know best in a situation and when we begin to pray prayers that control and try to change the situation to what we think should happen. It looks like this: "I'm not happy with the way my leader is leading so I'm going to pray that he changes and begins to do it the way I think he or she should do it." Can you see the error in that? As intercessors, our job is to support our leaders and to bless them, to come alongside and serve them. I love it when people come up to us and tell us that they are praying blessing for us and that they want to help in any way by serving us. Let's face it, our leaders need all of the help they can get. After all, they are human, too.

Many of us have unintentionally prayed these prayers. If you have been one to control with your prayers, just ask the Lord to forgive you and begin blessing those whom you have unintentionally cursed. Some have done so on purpose and need to repent and make a new start. You may need to personally commit to God that you will honor and begin serving your leaders.

Speaking Love

I have learned over the years that those who are critical toward leadership are often those who carry an intercessory gift. They need to turn their criticism into prayers. They need to pray the opposite of what they are speaking and stop living under the influence of the second realm. I would like to think that God cannot hear those words that are critical but that He can hear those words or prayers that are filled with blessing and love.

> *For you, brethren, have been called to liberty; only do not use liberty as an opportunity for the flesh, but through love serve one another* (Galatians 5:13).

> *Hope does not disappoint, because the **love** of God has been poured out within our hearts through the Holy Spirit who was given to us* (Romans 5:5 NASB).

There is a lot of love within our spirits, and we need to cultivate that love. As you tap into the love that is yours, you will begin to see people with God's loving eyes. Instead of praying or speaking words of death, you will begin to pray and speak words of life and love.

Stop right now and quiet your heart and feel His love—this love that gives us liberty as it destroys all fear, this love that gives us the freedom to love others.

A Warning

We were traveling and visiting a church back East. During one of the meetings, my husband had a word of knowledge about a woman having a stillbirth or a miscarriage. There were several women who stood for prayer. It felt like to me there were way too many standing. At lunch that day I was sitting next to the pastor's wife. I asked her about all the miscarriages and stillbirths that were going on. As she was telling me about what was going on, I felt impressed to ask her what the intercessors had been doing. I explained that there are times when we can participate in warfare that God has not ordained. She began to tell me that a while back they had partnered with a group of other intercessors and had gone up on a mountain called "Witch Mountain." They had rebuked the principality over that region. She told me she had felt apprehensive about doing such a thing but had joined in anyway.

As I listened to the pastor's wife explain the types of prayers her prayer teams had been praying, I began to get a picture of what had been taking place. I felt like the Lord showed me that what they did was not led of God. I believe they entered into an area in the spiritual realm where God had not sent them, and they ended up uncovered. The result was that there was a loss of life. So we came up with a plan for the meeting that night. To break this curse over the church, we called forward all of the women who could not get pregnant or had miscarried or had stillbirths. There was a whole line of women that night. Bill and I spent quite a while praying over each one of them. As Bill and I came to one young woman, she whispered in my ear, "I just found out that I'm pregnant." I felt like it was God saying, "This is the first fruit of the healing."

As intercessors, we need to be careful and sensitive to what God wants us to do. We are never to fear the devil. But we are also never to fight the devil on our own terms. If we let God direct and empower, there will always be advancement and victory. If you feel a hesitation in your spirit, then listen to that, and wait on the Lord. There have been times when I have set out to do some praying with all of the best intentions, and God has whispered to me, "not now" or "don't touch that in prayer." It's not to put fear in us and to stop the ministry of our intercessions, but we need to be wise and learn to listen and be sensitive to the moving of the Holy Spirit. God's grace is so big and wide and strong that when we make a mistake, we just repent and get up and keep going.

For Such a Time as This

All through history God has raised up an army of warriors that will lay down their lives for the cause. How many times has God woken you up and drawn you unto Himself for such a time as this? You may not always understand why, but you are to join Him. Let history belong to you, intercessor. Step into who you are and dive into the depths of His riches.

ENDNOTES

1. Renee Cooper, leader over Arts and Intercession at Bethel Church. Used by permission.

2. For more information, contact Pastor Eric Johnson, Bethel Church, Redding, California.

3. Taken from notes by Marla Baum, Intercessory Prayer leader at Bethel Church.

11

MYSTICS, MYSTICAL EXPERIENCES, AND CONTEMPLATIVE PRAYER

> True contemplatives do not seek
> unusual experiences, much less
> personal power. Their consuming
> goal is intimacy with God.
>
> —*Dame Julian of Norwich*

Your way, O God, is in the sanctuary (Psalm 77:13).

This chapter is dedicated to the mystics, the contemplatives, those now and those who have gone on before us, those who have lived in deep communion with the Three-ness, the Trinity. The mystics call their communion, "ecstasies." As you read this chapter, my hope and prayer is that you will experience the realms of ecstasy, the realms where you are called to the deep places of God, and that His water will flow over you.

I've found myself being drawn to learning as much as I can about the mystics. To me, "mystics" are the people who have laid down their entire lives to seek after one thing, the very heart of God. One of the things that make "mystics" different from other people is that they have only one desire, to know God in His fullness.

Mystics are people who live in right relationship with God and who have truly surrendered themselves to knowing Him more, no matter what the cost. Mystics do not seek after fame, glory, or worldly desires, but they have chosen instead to lay their entire lives down so that they can hear the heartbeat of Heaven. Mystics are people who have a continual awareness of God.

Mystics are not satisfied with what is in front of them. They want to see more. Mystics see beyond this reality and into the spirit realm.

To them, God is more real than life. God is their life. Mystics see how the spirit realm connects with the worldly realms. In other words, they see how and where Heaven is invading earth. They take all of those connections, and they put them together and make sense of it all. Mystics are able to see into the spiritual realm and use it to help define what is going on in the earthly realm. In this sense, they help to bring Heaven to earth.

To the mystic, the spirit realm is a safe place. To them, the spiritual realm can often seem more real than the earthly realm. In fact, a mystic thrives on experiencing that heavenly realm.

There are many different types of mystics. One of those types is what some call a *cave dweller*. The Desert Fathers who lived as hermits are often referred to as cave dwellers. A cave dweller likes to be alone with God and would spend all of his time alone with God if he could. Once, when I was traveling, I met a young man who I instantly knew was a cave dweller. I asked him, and he agreed that he was a cave dweller. I can't really explain how I knew that he was a cave dweller, but I could just tell. I could see it in his eyes and on his face and all around him in the spiritual realm. I could tell that he was one who preferred to spend his time alone with God. I could tell that he was a friend of God.

Another type of mystic is a seer. A seer is able to *see* into the spiritual realm and discern the times and seasons that we are living in. One example of that type of mystic is Bob Jones. Bob Jones is a seer prophet.

Connection With God

I know when I am really in that place where I feel completely connected to God because I have an instant peace. When I am in that place, it feels as though everything makes sense and becomes "centered" in an instant. In that place, I experience a peace and warmth that could be described as nothing but truly divine. It is almost saying "aahhh" in my spirit, soul, and body. There is nothing on earth that is like that feeling. It is pure ecstasy.

I have found that, because I have spent time in the presence of God and have learned how to access His presence, it has become easier for me to connect with God. And because I have developed that connection, when I turn my attention to God, I can immediately begin to feel His presence.

Because I know what it feels like to be connected with God, I have become much more aware of how it feels when I have lost that connection. I have learned that, when I am not walking in that connecting place with God where I feel His presence, I begin to feel insecure. The best way that I can describe this feeling is that, all of a sudden, everything begins to feel out of sorts, and I have to re-connect with the heart of God and His presence to make everything feel like it has fallen back into its right place again, and once things fall back into place, they become "rightly fitted."

Another way that I can tell if I'm not at that connecting place with God is that I begin to let outside influences affect my emotions, my spirit man, and my decisions because I am not connected to what is truly real. "While we do not look at the things which are seen, but at the things which are not seen, for the things which are seen are temporary, but the things which are not seen are eternal" (2 Cor. 4:18).

When we connect with God, we make ourselves aware that He is right there all the time. And I have learned that I can experience that reality of the presence of God no matter where I am or what I am doing. It is an awareness that He is right there when I am in my car, while I am taking a walk, or playing with my grandchildren. And because I have spent time with God, focusing on His presence, I have found that I now have access to an instant connection.

Mystics—Super and Natural

To me, the mystics are just normal people. They are normal people consumed by the presence of God. They are normal people who enjoy being with God and who know how to move in and out of the secret place.

I used to think of mystics as people who just stayed secluded with God and hid themselves away from other people and from the world. But many of the mystics did not stay secluded. In fact, a lot of them lived in the world and touched the world. Saints Patrick and Columba are examples of two mystics who chose to impact the world around them with the Kingdom of God. These two men were great evangelists who moved in signs and wonders. Although they lived for the heartbeat of Heaven, they also chose to bring the Kingdom of Heaven to the earth. They knew how to touch the Father's heart, yet they moved among the people and ministered. And a long time ago, I decided that, if they can do both, I can do both.

A lot of times, when people think of mystics, they think of secluded people who run away from everything, but that is not always the case. Some of the people whom I would describe as modern-day mystics live extremely normal lives. Some of the most mystical people I know today are able to function in the world around them, even though they spend much of their time living in the spiritual realm. They get their life and their breath from the secret place. The most important thing to them is seeking the face of God, and they have a desire and a passion to know what God is doing and to hear what He is saying. They are desperate to hear the heartbeat of Heaven. Without that connection with Heaven, they begin to feel unbalanced.

The mystics are no different than you and me. They are everyday people who have chosen to lay their lives down to seek after God. They do not limit God. Mystics seek after God with their whole hearts. They go before God and say, "God, you are all that I desire. No matter what it looks like, or what it costs me, I must have more of you." The heart cry of the mystic is, "Take the world but give me you."

In the Bible, King David was a mystic. David did things way before his time. For example, David opened up worship for everybody. He opened it up for people to worship and be with God in the tabernacle. He made worship available. He said, we can all do this.

A mystical person who is in a right relationship with God and humankind will naturally open the gates for other people to go to the same places in the spiritual realm that he or she has discovered. We see this in Psalm 27:4, when David cries, "One thing I have desired of the Lord, that will I seek: that I may dwell in the house of the Lord all of the days of my life, to behold the beauty of the Lord and to inquire in His temple."

There are so many things that we can glean from the life of David. When we read the Bible, we can see that David made a lot of mistakes. But Paul writes, quoting from the Old Testament, in Acts 13:22, about God saying of David, "I have found David the son of Jesse, a man after My own heart, who will do all My will." David was a man after the heart of God. He pursued the Lord and His presence and was desperate to intimately know the heart of God. David was just a man. But he had a heart after God. And David's heart after God had that mystical essence to it. We can see that in his writing of the Psalms, in his earnest desire to be one with his Maker and to be known by His God. This is the heart cry of the mystic: to be one with God.

The Oneness

When I spend time in the secret place, alone with God, I become so wrapped up in His presence that every other desire loses its importance to me. When I allow His presence to consume me, I surrender myself so completely to His will that my desires begin to line up with His. I become fully engulfed in His presence, lost in a sea of His beauty, and captivated by His love. In that place is the fullness of joy, the fullness of peace, the fullness of love, and the fullness of acceptance. In that place, I become one with Him. And in that place, I have found myself "caught up" in many different types of mystical experiences.

Mystical Experiences

God wants us to understand His world and His Kingdom. He wants us to know all about Him and to know Him intimately. He wants to tell us His secrets and to share His heart with us. Often, when we experience these things, they come through mystical experiences. Mystical experiences are often difficult for our earthly minds to comprehend. It is as though they come from another world, secrets whispered to us from above.

Several years ago in one of our services, I had an encounter with Heaven that I would describe as a mystical experience. During this experience, the Lord took me into a vision where I walked out onto a beautiful ridge. There was a soft light over the ridge. As I walked out onto this ridge, I saw, off to the right overlooking a vast valley, Jesus sitting. I looked into the valley. It went on forever. There seemed to be no end to the valley. In the valley were thousands of people just standing. The best way to describe them was that they looked like dead men walking. They had the form of humans but were empty inside. The funny thing is that they were all holding suitcases. As I looked on, I realized that they were starting to ascend to the top of the ridge one at a time. As the first man came up the ridge, he came and stood right in front of me. The feeling was that they were in desperate need, for they were dead inside. They needed someone to help them. But, at the same time, they didn't know that they needed help.

I looked over at Jesus and didn't understand why He wasn't coming to help. There was no verbal communication between Jesus, but we communicated spirit-to-Spirit, which I think of as Spirit talk. As I looked to Jesus, out from behind Him came flying the Holy Spirit. He was not in human form but in a blue white energy form. He was this amazing form of energy that flew in every direction. He came right to the dead man and began flying and swirling around him. Jesus communicated to me at that moment that it was my responsibility to help the man. What he had in his suitcase was the key for help. I reached down and opened the suitcase and pulled out clothing. The clothing was spirit clothing. It was destiny, his personal giftings, and who this man really was. I just began dressing him, and the Holy Spirit was equipping him by swirling around him. As I dressed him in who he was called to be, the death left him. He was alive in spirit. That was the end of the vision. The vision filled me with a lot of emotion. The thing that was impressed on me the most was my partnering with the Holy Spirit who is light and energy.

I've thought about that vision many times. I realize now that in the vision Jesus didn't do anything because He already had done it on the cross. The Holy Spirit came because the Holy Spirit was sent to help us. I learned in that vision that the Holy Spirit is wild and full of heavenly energy. He never stops. He is always on the move. I'm so thankful for that vision because it gave me more understanding of the Trinity. When God gives us visions and dreams, it is to give us instruction and revelation into His realm. It is to understand that deep realm of the Spirit. "I will give you the treasures of darkness and hidden riches of secret places that you may know that I, the Lord, who call you by your name, Am the God of Israel" (Isa. 45:3).

Let the Walls Come Down

Some people fear the intimate places of the Lord. They are afraid that God is not good and that He won't protect them. They fear the things of God and the spiritual realm. As a result, they put up walls to God because they are afraid. But when we come to a place where we truly believe that God is good, that He is our heavenly Father, we can put those fears aside and dive into new realms of the Spirit and begin to experience the fullness of the goodness of God.

Different Types of Prayer

There are so many different types of prayer and so many different ways to pray. I grew up believing that if I was going to pray, I had to use words. I have discovered that is only one form of prayer. There are many other forms of prayer. Often when I am in prayer, I do not use words at all. And sometimes when I am in that place, the Lord brings me into different types of prayer or intercessory experiences where the way that I pray begins to change. I do not go seeking these experiences out, but sometimes when I am in that place, they come upon me. Some of those different types of prayer include travail, brooding, ecstasies, and types of contemplative prayer.

Travail

One type of prayer is travail. *Travail* is a type of prayer where a person "labors" in prayer. A great example of travail is what Jesus did in the Garden of Gethsemane. In Luke 22:44 it says, "Being in agony, He prayed more earnestly. Then his sweat became like great drops of blood falling down to the ground." Travail is an intense feeling of giving birth to something. During travail, your prayers are deep cries and groans that come from your inner man. There are times when all that you can do is act out in a physical way what is happening in the spirit realm. These physical acts become prophetic. They become the very thing that will cause a release to come in what you are praying for.

It may be easier to describe what travail is with an example. One evening at church, Bill and I both noticed one of the young ladies who was having a difficult time. At the time, she was in close relationship with someone who had been diagnosed with cancer. The young lady came over to us and began to cry and shake. I knew immediately that she was moving into travail. I knew it was not something that she had picked because it is not in her personality at all. I explained to her what was happening and told her that she was in travail. I prayed with her through the entire process and let her travail through the rest of the worship service. I sat with her as deep groans came up out of her. After a little while, I knew that she needed to be released from the travail, and I told her to release the prayer burden that she was experiencing back to God. As soon as she released the burden back to God, you could see the release come over her. The young lady asked me if she could use one of the flags and go up on the platform. This was so out of character for her that I knew it was God. She went up on stage and used the flag as worship. When she did this, I felt like there was a release for her and that this was something she needed to do—something in the physical realm as the fruit of what had just happened in the spiritual realm. She did not carry that travail or the heaviness anymore; she had released it and given it to God.

Let me give you another example of travail. James Goll, an itinerant minister, was visiting our church years ago for a conference. During the conference, James came up to me and called me a weeping intercessor. At that point in my life, it was like refreshing water to my spirit to hear those words. He was right when he called it out to me. I felt like that was all I was doing, just crying in travail all of the time. I was asking God, "Why am I doing all this crying?" Many of us feel God in different ways. And sometimes we show physical manifestations of those feelings. When I feel God, I usually cry. It could have been because I was feeling His joy and I was crying tears of joy, or sometimes I was feeling His strong presence and His desire or His love for the world. Feeling His love for this world is a very intense feeling and will undo you every time. His love is vast and great and those words don't come close to describing His love for us.

Sometimes, when a person is in travail, it can almost appear as if she is in the process of childbirth. I remember a lot of people were falling into travailing prayer during the late '90s when there was so much change that was taking place in the spiritual atmosphere of the Church. I could feel it all. It was amazing to feel and see what God was doing. It was a pushing in the spiritual realm. At the church, we were having prayer meetings during the week. There were meetings that were filled with travail and great celebration. People in the church could feel what was happening. I don't know if we understood all that was happening, but we knew that God was doing something really big. There were physical prophetic acts of labor at times in these meetings. It looked as though they were birthing the things of the Lord in their prayers. Some people would have what we affectionately called "the crunches." In one of our services I remember there were several of us women who began to double over with labor type symptoms. It looked like we were having contractions.

During that season, we spent hours laughing and crying together. Little did we know what God would be establishing in the years to come. We felt it but didn't have complete definition for it.

Travail is a deep calling in your spirit. Everything in you is exploding with groanings that words can't express. It shakes your very core. Psalm 42:7 says:

Deep calls to deep at the sound of Your waterfalls; All Your breakers and Your waves have rolled over me (NASB).

Think about this verse. God's sound, like waterfalls, has called you to the deep place; all of His breakers and waves roll over you. If and when this happens, you become a mess. You become a complete mess for God. It makes you cry out for God all the more. Unfortunately, some people can let themselves stay in that place of travail long after the Lord has called them to it. If they are not careful, they can and will carry the feelings of that realm and turn them into soul feelings, which will only lead to sorrow. I can't tell you how many intercessors have ended up consumed by worldly sorrow. We have to understand that the devil does not play fair. He will take a very anointed time and twist it and turn it, and you will find yourself in a state of depression because you carried sorrow for too long. In short, something birthed by the Spirit can become fleshly if we are not careful.

Brooding

There are times when the Holy Spirit gives us specific things to pray for. And they won't go away. That is *brooding,* a type of prayer where we "sit on" or "ponder over" an issue that we are praying about.

I thought I would use this prayer tool one day when I had a mother come to me and ask for prayer for her son who was in prison. He needed God. So I shared with her about this brooding of the Holy Spirit. We prayed and asked that the Holy Spirit would come and brood over and around him, to cause life to come to him. A short time after that, she came back to me and told me that her son had given his life to the Lord. I remember thinking, "That was fast." So, I began using that whenever a parent would come and ask for prayer for a child. On one occasion, I had a father come who was so broken over his daughter's choices for her life. She had turned away from God. As we prayed, we released the Holy Spirit to come and brood over her so that she would feel the presence of the Holy Spirit. He came to me the next week with a great report. He had met with her after a week, and they went for a walk. She opened up and told him, "I don't know what you did, Dad, but I have felt God this week. It is like He is right next to me."

When the Holy Spirit "moves" over void, empty things, life can be the only result. When we are in this place of brooding, we stay very focused in our prayers. We are driven by Heaven to see an answer come.

> *The earth was without form, and void; and darkness was on the face of the deep. And the Spirit of God was hovering over the face of the waters* (Genesis 1:2).

When we brood, we bring the issues "under our wings" so to speak and keep them close to our hearts and pray until the birth comes. In his book *Intercessory Prayer*, Dutch Sheets gives a great word study on the word *hovering*.[1] It is a creative word. When the Holy Spirit "hovered" or "moved" or "brooded over," it produced life where there was void, nothingness. The word *hover* is used as a term for when a hen broods over her chicks.

Baby Chicks

Let me tell you a story to illustrate this brooding prayer. Years ago, when our children were young, we decided that we would raise some chickens. It was so much fun. The kids and I would race to the pen to see how many eggs we could collect. One morning I noticed that one of the hens was sitting on her eggs. So every morning, we would look inside the nest to see the progress. We were so excited and waited anxiously for the new chicks. One very cold morning as I walked into the pen, the mama hen stood up and out from her wings fell two little chicks. She had birthed them, and they were amazing. I think about that picture often when it comes to prayer. Many times that is what we are doing when we intercede. We are brooding over something, causing life to come. I never saw those eggs while that mama was sitting. They were hidden away. It was a secret place. That hen was protecting those chicks with all of her might. Can you see the joy of anticipation in the brooding process? Yes it's work and it takes endurance, but there is an excitement because you know that the answer is coming. That mama hen just sat and waited. We do the same. We wait and protect, creating the atmosphere that enables the birth to happen. What joy!

Cause and Effect

I had a friend come to me and tell me that she saw that I was praying for three things. The picture she saw was of a hen that was brooding over her eggs. When she told me this, it helped me identify what I was feeling about three different things that I had been praying about. I was producing or creating something in my prayers that was causing life to come, that was causing an answer. It's cause and effect. Cause and effect—the way perspectives, objectives, and/or measures interact in a series of cause-and-effect relationships—demonstrates the impact of achieving an outcome. You are the right person at the right time causing increase as you pray. Many times intercessors feel that they are hovering over an issue that the Father is birthing in them. They can actually feel the life coming as they pray.

Sometimes the Holy Spirit will have us "brood over" a topic that we are praying about. For me, a lot of the things that I find myself "brooding over" are issues of more global concern. When this happens, God will release prayer strategies to me little by little, and I will sit on that thing until I see the answer. And I know when it has been "birthed" because I see the answer come. Sometimes, what I see is a process of answers or a progression of answered prayer. For example, sometimes I will hear about an answer of something that I have been brooding over in a news story or in a casual conversation. I make sure that, when I am brooding over something, I continually look for an answer because I know that God always answers my prayers. I expect it.

Breath Prayers

There are some prayers that seem to come up out of your inner man. I call these *breath prayers*. They're not long prayers, but they are spirit-breathed. Many times when I soak in God's presence, I will experience this breath. It will start deep inside of me and stir me to where my own breath is taken away. Many times there are no words that come, only breathing Him in and breathing my prayers out.

A Thin Place

A *thin place* is a place where Heaven and earth are close. It is easier to experience the spiritual realm in these places. A lot of times, you can tell when you are in a "thin place" because there are a lot of spiritual or creative people who are gathered there. Examples of this include Sedona, Arizona; Ashland, Oregon; and many parts of Ireland, which is known for its thin places. In contemplative prayer, you discover that the atmosphere around you becomes thin to the point that there is no division between Heaven and earth. A friend and I were walking down a trail one day to visit a water site that we wanted to pray at. We were praying as we walked. Both of us at the same time ran right into a thin place. We both stopped and said, "Wow. Do you feel that?" We felt like we had just entered into a place where our world and the realm of Heaven collided. We got so drunk in the Spirit from walking into that thin place that we could hardly make it the rest of the way down the trial.

Dark Night of the Soul

There are times in our lives that we go through really hard stuff. We can do one of two things: run away from God or run to Him. I've found that running to Him is the only answer. During this *dark night of the soul* God allows us to come to a brokenness that brings us to complete surrender. If we turn to Him in surrender and release everything to Him, a peace will come and settle deep in us. It will feel like an oil of healing being poured over and in us. The sweetness of this peace will take away the brokenness.

There are other times that we are in great travail over something. The burden of this can feel so overpowering that we feel as though we could die. These are times that we need to stay very close and continually give Him the burden. We need to turn the dark night of the soul over to Him. The world doesn't need our sadness; they need our joy.

Ecstasies

An *ecstasy* could be defined as a period of time in prayer when the awareness of the soul is suspended and the only focus that the person has is the incredible presence of the Lord.

Sometimes my only prayer is, "God I want to be one with you." The only desire of my heart is to know Him and be known by Him. When I am in that place, sometimes I find myself slipping into the ecstasies of God. When I slip into the ecstasies of God, I slip into an eternal realm where I become so consumed by the presence of God that it feels like I cease to exist outside of His goodness. In that place, I become completely consumed by Him. In that place, I become completely known by Him. In that place, I become one with Him.

One mystic who was often swept up into "ecstasies" was St. Teresa of Avila. Author of (among other books and writings) *Interior Castle*, a classic book about union with God and contemplative prayer, Teresa of Avila was a Spanish mystic who lived from 1515-1582. Here is how she described her experience of union with God:

> *It pleased our Lord that I should see the following vision a number of times. I saw an angel near me, on the left side, in bodily form. This I am not wont to see, save very rarely.... In this vision it pleased the Lord that I should see it thus. He was not tall, but short, marvelously beautiful, with a face which shone as though he were one of the highest of the angels, who seem to be all of fire: they must be those whom we call Seraphim.... I saw in his hands a long golden spear, and at the point of the iron there seemed to be a little fire. This I thought that he thrust several times into my heart, and that it penetrated to my entrails. When he drew out the spear he seemed to be drawing them with it, leaving me all on fire with a wondrous love for God. The pain was so great that it caused me to utter several moans; and yet so exceeding sweet is this greatest of pains that it is*

impossible to desire to be rid of it, or for the soul to be content with less than God.[2]

Contemplative Prayer

Contemplative prayer is an inner prayer, a spirit-to-spirit prayer, a form of meditation, a dwelling on Him. I could also define contemplative prayer as an awareness of God. A lot of the different types of prayer already mentioned in this book are types of contemplative prayer. When I am in a place of contemplative prayer, I would say that I am in a place where I am aware of the presence of God.

I find myself falling into contemplative prayer when I quiet myself before God, and I start by just adoring Him. For me, I simply behold the goodness of God, and I find myself slipping away with Him. I don't get there by stress or striving; it is simply by surrendering to His presence.

> Reading seeks, meditation finds (meaning), prayer demands, contemplation tastes (God).
>
> Reading provides solid food, meditation masticates (chews); prayer achieves a savor; contemplation is the sweetness that refreshes.
>
> Reading is on the surface; meditation gets to the inner substance; prayer demands by desire; contemplation experiences by delight.
>
> —*Teresa of Avila*[3]

Some people, when contemplating God, will take a verse or word pertaining to God, like His greatness, and begin to meditate on it. As they put themselves in this quiet place, they begin to have an awareness of God and His presence indwelling them. This is where words aren't important anymore; it's communication of the Spirit kind. There are many who, from this place, will begin to have heavenly experiences.

Meditation

Formal Christian meditation began with the early Christian monastic practice of reading the Bible slowly. Monks would carefully consider the deeper meaning of each verse as they read it. This slow and thoughtful reading of Scripture, and the ensuing pondering of its meaning, was their meditation. This spiritual practice is called "divine reading," or *lectio divina*.

Sometimes the monks found themselves spontaneously praying as a result of their meditation on Scripture, and their prayer would in turn lead on to a simple, loving focus on God. This wordless love for God they called contemplation.

The progression from Bible reading, to meditation, to prayer, to loving regard for God, was first formally described by Guigo II, a Carthusian monk and prior of Grande Chartreuse in the 12th century. Guigo named the four steps of this "ladder" of prayer with the Latin terms lectio, meditatio, oratio, and contemplatio.[4]

All of these people had the same thing in common: a passion and fire within to seek after God. We can't be afraid to enter this realm with God. We can't be afraid that it might be something demonic. For years in the Church, meditation has been misunderstood as something that belongs only to different cults. Listen, many of the things in cults are just perversions of the real. The practice meditation, in many cults, is the practice of emptying our head of all things. That is what they call meditation. As believers, when we meditate on the Lord, we are actually filling our heads with the wonders of God and His greatness.

> *Be angry, and do not sin. Meditate within your heart on your bed, and be still. Selah* (Psalm 4:4).

By now you have figured out that having an intimate relationship with the Three-ness, the Holy Trinity, is vital in an intercessor's life. We must learn to know the Father, the Son, and the Holy Spirit. Being righteous is being in right standing with God, the Trinity. The Bible says that the effective, fervent prayers of a righteous man avails (profits) much (see James 5:16). The *Message Bible* says it this way: "The prayer of a person living right with God is something powerful to be reckoned with." We must have an ongoing relationship with the Trinity and be constant in our pursuit of this heavenly presence. We must experience the Godhead.

Lose Yourself in Him

All of the words in this book come down to one thing: time spent with God. There is a place in all of us that cannot be filled with anything but God. It's a deep place for us to dwell with our heavenly Father. In order for us to get to this place, we must quiet ourselves inside and learn to know and feel Him.

Tonight, as you lay your head on your pillow, let all of the stuff from your day just fall off, and begin to think on Him. Meditate in your heart about His goodness. Read a verse or pick a word that describes Him and begin to connect your spirit with His. Take some time and practice being still before Him. Words won't be necessary. One of the proposed meanings of the word *selah* is "to pause and ponder." Ponder the things of God. As you practice this, you will soon be lost and caught up in His presence. You will begin to understand His world.

ENDNOTES

1. Dutch Sheets, *Intercessory Prayer* (Ventura, CA: Regal Books, 1996), 157.

2. Teresa of Avila, quoted in Allison E. Peers, *Studies of the Spanish Mystics*, Vol. 1 (New York: The Macmillan Co., 1927), 197.

3. "Teresa of Avila Lectio," http://www.prayingchurch.org/teresa.html (accessed 13 April 2008).

4. "Christian Meditation," http://en.wikipedia.org/wiki/Christian_meditation (accessed 13 April 2008).

QUESTIONS ON PRAYER AND INTERCESSION

1. The Bible doesn't mention an official position of an intercessor. Where did we, as Christians today, get this from?

Even though the Bible doesn't have an official title for an intercessor, there are many examples in the Bible of times when God looked for an intercessor.

In Isaiah 59:16, it says "He saw that there was no man, And wondered that there was no intercessor; therefore His own arm brought salvation for Him; and His own righteousness, it sustained Him." Then again in Ezekiel 22:30, "So I sought for a man among them who would make a wall, and stand in the gap before Me on behalf of the land, that I should not destroy it; but I found no one."

Many people, especially the prophets in the Bible, defined *intercessor* for us through their lives, even though they were not given that title. One of those would be Moses. Moses stood before God on many occasions to ask God for mercy on behalf of a stiff-necked people. On one occasion, God told Moses that He would change His mind because of him (see Num. 14:20).

God looks for those who will stand in the gap for whatever the reason. Another thing demonstrated in these verses is that God really does want us to partner with Him for His Kingdom.

2. What is the difference between prayer and intercession?

Prayer in the Old Testament is the same word as *intercession*, for the most part. In the New Testament, the word *prayer* means "to worship, to petition, or make a request." The definition of the word *intercession*, in the New Testament, is very similar to *prayer*:

> The word, *paga*, translated intercession, in the Old Testament means "by accident or violence, cause to entreat, fall, light upon, meet together."[1]

There is not much difference between the two, except for the violent (*paga*) part of intercession. That would involve a more intense part of prayer.

I believe that intercession is the action of pleading on somebody's behalf, the action of attempting to settle a dispute or a prayer to God, a god, or a saint on behalf of somebody or something.

To intercede is to plead with somebody in authority on behalf of somebody else, especially somebody who is to be punished for something. It is to speak in support of somebody involved in a dispute; it is an attempt to settle a dispute between others.

Intercession involves reaching God, meeting God, and entreating Him for His favor.

3. Are we all called to pray and intercede?

Yes, we are. We are all called to have a relationship with our Father. And out of that, it should be automatic for us to pray. But I do believe that a person can have a gift of intercession. It would be a gift given by God. You can tell that you have this gift if all that you want to do is be with God and if you feel yourself being pulled into prayer by what you see around you.

4. Why pray?

Remember, prayer is talking to God. I love being around my husband. We have a wonderful relationship. We spend time together and talk and share our lives. I feel that God is looking for those who will commune (talk) with Him and be with Him. He is our Father and does want to share His heart with us. As He shares, we in response will want to pray. It is a partnering.

> *Rejoice always, pray without ceasing, in everything give thanks; for this is the will of God in Christ Jesus for you* (1 Thessalonians 5:16-17).

The Bible does tell us that it is God's will for our lives.

5. How long does one have to pray for a particular issue?

From my own experience, I believe that there are life assignments that God gives each of us. For me, that is praying for the five-fold government of the Church to be set up and in working order. But, I also think that God gives us short-term prayer assignments. How do you know when that assignment is over? You will feel a lifting or release from the assignment.

There are also times when an assignment will come and go. For example, for several years I had been praying for a particular region and even for a specific leader in that region. Then, it all stopped for a year. One morning I woke up and thought, "I wonder how that person is doing?" The desire to pray for this region and person all came back, and I began to pray again. I think the key here is to be sensitive to His voice, and you will know.

6. How do we know that we are praying to God's will?

To be honest there are times when we hit and miss, and from that, we learn how to know. We always must use the Bible for a guideline as well.

"In the same way the Spirit also helps our weakness; for we do not know how to pray as we should, but the Spirit Himself intercedes for us with groanings too deep for words" (Romans 8:26). The spirit in a man knows the man, so with the Holy Spirit. He knows the Father. So if we are tapped into the Holy Spirit, we will have a much higher percentage of our prayers being right on track.

We need to be careful that we are not manipulating with our prayers. I have addressed this in Chapter 10.

7. When should we travail in prayer?

For me, travailing is not something I choose. It chooses me.

8. What about praying in the Spirit; how does praying in tongues become intercession?

For an intercessor, tongues play an important role as we pray. I spend a lot of time praying in tongues. I like to use my prayer language when I take walks. As I walk, I begin praying in tongues, and I can feel my spirit begin to engage with the Holy Spirit. As I continue to pray, things will come to my mind, and I will speak in tongues over those things. It can become easy to speak in tongues and not engage with Holy Spirit. It can become just something we do with no life on it. But engaging with our spirit language causes our prayers to become effective.

I had a friend come to me and ask for prayer. As I began praying for her, I felt like I was to speak into her ear and pray in tongues. As I began praying in tongues over her, both of us felt our spirits engaging with the tongue. She was able to receive and get breakthrough in what she was going through.

9. Intercession and decrees. What is a decree?

I believe that there are two ways to pray. One is petition, which is making a request and the other is the declaration, which comes from a place of faith or belief that it will be done. I feel that many intercessors are really good at petitioning, but that they don't know how to move into a place of faith, knowing that it is time to declare a thing as done. Several years ago, I felt like it was time for us to begin to make declarations and to stop petitioning so much in our prayers. Our focus needed to shift from the posture of making requests before God to a posture of faith and taking the authority that is ours. I actually felt that there was a shift in our authority level. Because we had petitioned for so long, it was a time for us to begin declaring things into being.

When we take teams out to pray, I will tell them, "I want you to make a declaration or decree over this land." It would be similar to giving a prophetic word. You are using your words of declaration to cause a change.

10.   What are some tips for praying in a group?

When you call people together, you are going to have all different kinds of prayers. Some will be ready to violently go after God, and others will want to quietly pray, while others may want to have a list of things to pray over. As a leader, you need to set some ground rules. For example, when praying for a topic, you want to make sure that you exhaust the subject in praying before you go on to another. In many meetings, when someone starts out praying for something and then the next person moves on to something different, you haven't exhausted the prayer. There may be more that someone else wanted to pray. You want to make sure that everyone prays and completes the prayer before moving on to another topic.

Tell people in the group that they need to give everyone a chance to pray and that one or two people should not take over the prayer meeting.

I have found that the best way to bring a whole group together in prayer is to have them all soak in God's presence first. This brings everyone into the heart of God, and after soaking, you will find the prayer time to be much more rewarding and effective.

ENDNOTE

1. *New American Standard Exhaustive Concordance of the Bible, Hebrew-Aramaic and Greek Dictionary*, Robert L. Thomas, Ed., version 2.2, s.v. "Paga."

Appendix

A Big Dose of Joy

Joy means "a feeling of great happiness or pleasure, especially of an elevated or spiritual kind." There are other words that associate with the word *joy*: delight, happiness, pleasure, bliss, ecstasy, elation, and thrill. The word *ecstasy* means "a feeling of intense delight." The word *bliss* means "perfect untroubled happiness."[1]

The word *joy* is in the Bible 182 times. I have picked out several references on joy for you to read. I feel that it is important to include these verses in this book. They are reminders to us of the importance of being a joyful people, of being who we were created to be. Not only that, but it is important that we as believers represent, or re-present, who our heavenly Father is here on earth. He is loving and joyful. He laughs from Heaven. Most of the verses have several translations for your enjoyment.

Psalm 21:6—*For You make him most blessed forever; You make him joyful with gladness in Your presence* (NASB).

Psalm 68:3—*But let the righteous be glad; let them exult before God; yes, let them rejoice with gladness* (NASB).

Psalm 100:2—*Serve the Lord with gladness; come before Him with joyful singing* (NASB).

Gladness is experiencing joy and pleasure. In these verses, we see that being in God's presence brings gladness.

Isaiah 55:12—*For you will go out with joy And be led forth with peace; the mountains and the hills will break forth into shouts of joy before you, and all the trees of the field will clap their hands* (NASB).

Isaiah 55:12—*For you shall go out with joy, and be led forth with peace: the mountains and the hills shall break forth before you into singing; and all the trees of the fields shall clap their hands* (WEB).

Isaiah 55:12—*For you shall go out in joy, and be led back in peace; the mountains and the hills before you shall burst into song, and all the trees of the field shall clap their hands* (NRSV).

Isaiah 55:12—*So you'll go out in joy, you'll be led into a whole and complete life. The mountains and hills will lead the parade, bursting with song. All the trees of the forest will join the procession, exuberant with applause* (TM).

Jeremiah 15:16—*Your words were found and I ate them, and Your words became for me a joy and the delight of my heart; for I have been called by Your name, O Lord God of hosts* (NASB).

Jeremiah 15:16—*Your words were found, and I ate them, and Your word was to me the joy and rejoicing of my heart; for I am called by Your name, O Lord God of hosts* (NKJV).

Jeremiah 15:16—*When your words showed up, I ate them—swallowed them whole. What a feast! What delight I took in being yours, O God, God of-the-Angel-Armies* (TM).

Zephaniah 3:17—*The Lord your God is in your midst, a victorious warrior. He will exult over you with joy, He will be quiet in His love, He will rejoice over you with shouts of joy* (NASB).

Zephaniah 3:17—*The Lord your God in your midst, the Mighty One, will save; He will rejoice over you with gladness, He will quiet you with His love, He will rejoice over you with singing* (NKJV).

Zephaniah 3:17—*The Lord, your God, is in your midst, a warrior who gives victory; He will rejoice over you with gladness, He will renew you in His love; He will exult over you with loud singing* (NRSV).

Zephaniah 3:17—*Your God is present among you, a strong Warrior there to save you. Happy to have you back,*

He'll calm you with His love and delight you with His songs (TM).

Zechariah 8:19—*Thus says the Lord of hosts, "The fast of the fourth, the fast of the fifth, the fast of the seventh and the fast of the tenth months will become **joy**, gladness, and cheerful feasts for the house of Judah; so love truth and peace"* (NASB).

John 15:11—*These things I have spoken to you so that My joy may be in you, and that your joy may be made full* (NASB).

John 15:11—*I've told you these things for a purpose: that My joy might be your joy, and your joy wholly mature* (TM).

John 15:11—*I have said these things to you so that My joy may be in you, and that your joy may be complete* (NRSV).

John 15:11—*These things I have spoken to you, that My joy in you may remain, and your joy may be full* (YLT).

John 15:11—*I have spoken these things to you that My joy may be in you, and your joy be full* (DRBY).

John 17:13—*But now I come to You, and these things I speak in the world, that they may have My joy fulfilled in themselves* (NKJV).

John 17:13—*But now I come to You; and these things I speak in the world so that they may have My joy made full in themselves* (NASB).

John 17:13—*Now I'm returning to you. I'm saying these things in the world's hearing. So My people can experience My joy completed in them* (TM).

Acts 13:52—*And the disciples were continually filled with **joy** and with the Holy Spirit* (NASB).

Acts 13:52—*Brimming with joy and the Holy Spirit, two happy disciples* (TM).

Acts 13:52—*The disciples were filled with joy with the Holy Spirit* (WEB).

Acts 2:28—*You have made known to me the ways of life; You will make me full of gladness with Your presence* (NASB).

Acts 15:3—*Therefore, being sent on their way by the church, they were passing Through both Phoenicia and Samaria, describing in detail the conversion of the Gentiles, and were bringing great **joy** to all the brethren* (NASB).

Acts 15:3—*After they were sent off and on their way, they told everyone they met as they traveled through Phoenicia and Samaria about the breakthrough to the Gentile outsiders. Everyone who heard the news cheered—it was terrific news* (TM).

Acts 15:3—*They, being sent on their way by the assembly, passed through both Phoenicia and Samaria, declaring the conversion of the Gentiles. They caused great joy to all the brothers* (WEB).

Romans 14:17—*For the kingdom of God is not eating and drinking, but righteousness and peace and **joy** in the Holy Spirit* (NASB).

Romans 14:17—*For the kingdom of God is not eating and drinking, but righteousness, and peace, and joy in* [the] *Holy Spirit* (DRBY).

Romans 14:17—*God's kingdom isn't a matter of what you put in your stomach, for goodness' sake. It's what God does with your life as He sets it right, puts it together, and completes it with joy* (TM).

Romans 15:13—*Now may the God of hope fill you with all **joy** and peace in believing, so that you will abound in hope by the power of the Holy Spirit* (NASB).

Romans 15:13—*Oh! May the God of green hope fill you up with joy, fill you up with peace, so that your believing lives, filled with the life-giving energy of the Holy Spirit, will brim over with hope* (TM).

Romans 15:13—*and the God of the hope shall fill you with all joy and peace in the believing, for your abounding in the hope in power of the Holy Spirit* (YNG).

Psalms 51:12—*Restore to me the **joy** of Your salvation and sustain me with a willing spirit* (NAS).

Psalm 51:12—*Restore unto me the joy of Thy salvation; and uphold me with a willing spirit* (ASV).

Psalm 51:12—*Restore to me the joy of Thy salvation, and a willing spirit doth sustain me* (YNG).

Psalm 51:12—*Bring me back from gray exile, put a fresh wind in my sails* (TM).

Psalm 16:11—*You will make known to me the path of life; in Your presence is Fullness of joy; in Your right hand there are pleasures forever* (NASB).

Psalm 16:11—*Thou causest me to know the path of life; Fullness of joys [is] with Thy presence, pleasant things by Thy right hand forever!* (YNG)

Psalm 16:11—*Thou wilt make known to me the path of life: Thy countenance is fulness of joy; at thy right hand are pleasures for evermore* (DRBY).

Nehemiah 8:10—*Then he said to them, "Go, eat of the fat, drink of the sweet, and send portions to him who has nothing prepared; for this day is holy to our Lord. Do not be grieved, for the joy of the Lord is strength"* (NASB).

Nehemiah 8:10—*Then he said to them, "Go your way, eat the fat and drink sweet wine and send portions of them to those for whom nothing is prepared, for this day is* *holy to our Lord; and do not be grieved, for the joy of the Lord is your strength"* (NRSV).

Nehemiah 8:10—*And he saith to them, "Go, eat fat things, and drink sweet things, and sent portions to him for whom nothing is prepared, for to-day [is] holy to our Lord, and be not grieved, for the joy of Jehovah is your strength"* (YNG).

Nehemiah 8:10—*He continued, "Go home and prepare a feast, holiday food and drink; and share it with those who don't have anything: This day is holy to God. Don't feel bad. The joy of God is your strength"* (TM).

1 Chronicles 16:27—*Splendor and majesty are before Him, strength and **joy** are in His place* (NASB).

1 Chronicles 16:27—*Splendor and majesty flow out of Him, strength and joy fill His place* (TM).

1 Chronicles 16:27—*Splendor and majesty are before Him; strength and joy in His dwelling place* (NIV).

1 Chronicles 16:27—*Honor and majesty are before Him: Strength and gladness are in His place* (ASV).

Matthew 25:21—*His master said to him, "Well done, good and faithful slave. You were faithful with a few things, I will put you in charge of many things; **enter into the joy** of your master"* (NASB).

Matthew 25:21—*His master replied, "Well done, good and faithful servant! You have been faithful with a few things; I will put you in charge of many things. Come and share your master's happiness"* (NIV).

Hebrews 12:2—*Let us fix our eyes on Jesus, the author and perfecter of our faith, who for the joy set before Him endured the cross, scorning its shame, and sat down at the right hand of the throne of God* (NIV).

Hebrews 12:2—*Looking steadfastly on Jesus the leader and completer of faith: who, in view of the joy lying before Him, endured* [the] *cross, having despised* [the] *shame, and is set down at the right hand of the throne of God* (DRBY).

Hebrews 12:2—*looking to the author and perfecter of faith—Jesus, who, over against the joy set before Him— did endure a cross, shame having despised, on the right hand also of the throne of God did sit down* (YNG).

Hebrews 12:2—*Looking to Jesus the pioneer and perfecter of our faith, who for the sake of the joy that was set before Him endured the cross...* (NKJV).

ENDNOTE

1. *The New Webster Encyclopedic Dictionary of the English Language*, s.v.v. "Joy," "Ecstasy," "Bliss."

To contact the author please visit:

www.benij.org
www.happyintercessor.com
www.ibethel.org

Recommended Reading

❖ *A Life of Miracles* by Bill Johnson

❖ *Basic Training for the Prophetic Ministry* by Kris Vallotton

❖ *Basic Training for the Supernatural Ways of Royalty* by
Kris Vallotton

❖ *Developing a Supernatural Lifestyle* by Kris Vallotton

❖ *Dreaming With God* by Bill Johnson

❖ *Face to Face* by Bill Johnson

- *Here Comes Heaven* by Bill Johnson and Mike Seth

- *Loving Our Kids on Purpose* by Danny Silk

- *Purity* by Kris Vallotton

- *Strengthen Yourself in the Lord* by Bill Johnson

- *The Supernatural Power of a Transformed Mind* by Bill Johnson

- *The Supernatural Ways of Royalty* by Kris Vallotton and Bill Johnson

- *The Ultimate Treasure Hunt* by Kevin Dedmon

- *When Heaven Invades Earth* by Bill Johnson

Additional copies of this book and other
book titles from DESTINY IMAGE are
available at your local bookstore.

Call toll-free: 1-800-722-6774.

Send a request for a catalog to:

Destiny Image® Publishers, Inc.

P.O. Box 310
Shippensburg, PA 17257-0310

*"Speaking to the Purposes of God for this
Generation and for the Generations to Come."*

**For a complete list of our titles,
visit us at www.destinyimage.com.**